Tiny Worlds in Fabric

Sew Enchanting Fairy Houses & Miniature Masterpieces

Ramune Jauniskis

C&T PUBLISHING
Another Maker Inspired!

Text and photography copyright © 2022 by Ramune Jauniskis

Photography and artwork copyright © 2022 by C&T Publishing, Inc.

Publisher: Amy Barrett-Daffin

Creative Director: Gailen Runge

Editor: Liz Aneloski

Technical Editor: Helen Frost

Cover/Book Designer: April Mostek

Production Coordinator: Zinnia Heinzmann

Illustrator: Mary E. Flynn

Photography Coordinator: Lauren Herberg

Photography Assistant: Gabriel Martinez

Front cover and lifestyle photography by Francine Zaslow

Subjects and instructional photography by Ramune Jauniskis,
unless otherwise noted

Design elements: tip/note pattern by RODINA OLENA, background texture by
Magenta10m, flowers by lisima

Published by C&T Publishing, Inc., P.O. Box 1456, Lafayette, CA 94549

Library of Congress Cataloging-in-Publication Data

Names: Jauniskis, Ramune, 1960- author.
Title: Tiny worlds in fabric : sew enchanting fairy houses & miniature
    masterpieces / Ramune Jauniskis.
Description: Lafayette, CA : C&T Publishing, [2022] | Summary: "Use fabric
    fusing with fast2fuse to create enchanting works of art. Create 22
    whimsical treasures with full instructions and step-by-step photos to
    make these whimsical creations for crafters from beginners to
    experienced"-- Provided by publisher.
Identifiers: LCCN 2022036270 | ISBN 9781644031667 (trade paperback) | ISBN
    9781644031674 (ebook)
Subjects: LCSH: Textile crafts. | Miniature objects. | Fairies in art.
Classification: LCC TT699 .J38 2022 | DDC 746--dc23/eng/20220819
LC record available at https://lccn.loc.gov/2022036270

Printed in the USA

10 9 8 7 6 5 4 3 2 1

Dedication
For my parents

Acknowledgments

Thank you to everyone that helped me
with this book, my family members and friends
who supported me and cheered me on,
C&T Publishing for their patience,
Elise Flores for the countless times
that she helped me
with my writing and grammar,
and Salley Mavor
for her kind support.

Contents

12

18

42

46

74

82

50

70

86

Introduction

Although I have been working in the art field professionally for over 37 years, my love for creativity began long before that. I remember drooling over a set of 64 Pentel markers that my mother bought for me from a Spencer Gifts catalog. I surprised her by decorating my new white Keds with them. I was (and still am) always happiest when I'm creating. I'm so grateful for the opportunity to share my passion with others.

There really is no right or wrong way to create. This book is meant to give you guidance and inspiration. The directions and suggestions are meant as guides, not rules. I encourage everyone to follow their own inspiration and creativity. Some of the projects require working on a very small scale. It may seem impossible at first, but if you play around with the supplies and shapes, you will find it gets easier rather quickly. I have huge hands and I surprise myself (and others) when I make these tiny creations.

Although it's tempting to skip over the Getting Started chapter (I know I would), it is important to read, since it gives some tips that may make the projects easier.

This book consists of some of my favorite projects. The collapsible portable dollhouse is easy to make and store. The furniture is really fun to make; plus, it looks so cute when it's finished. The neighborhood fairies will appreciate the fairy houses. And, what better way to celebrate a birthday than with a cake candle holder or a wedding than with a bride and groom mermaid cake topper?

Getting Started

Wait...Stop...Read This First!

If you're like me, you will try to skip this section,
but it's really better if you read this before starting.

General Instructions and Tips

❋ Read the directions for each project *before* starting.

❋ Most of the patterns in this book are full-size; others larger ones will need to be enlarged. Enlarge them on a photocopy machine using the enlargement percentage given for each template pattern, or, you can download the full-size template patterns using the following link. To access ALL the full-size patterns for this book, type the web address below into your browser window.

tinyurl.com/11469-patterns-download

❋ Trace the patterns on cardstock or light-weight posterboard and cut them out. It takes a little longer, but this makes it so much easier to trace the shapes onto the fabric. You could also print them directly onto cardstock.

❋ Trace the shapes on the backing fabric side of the fabric sandwich since it will be easier to see the lines for cutting. Reverse one of each pair of mirrored pattern pieces.

❋ When tracing the shapes onto the fabric, draw the pieces with straight edges side by side for less cutting.

❋ Use any sewing machine with straight and zigzag stitches.

❋ Use a wide, dense zigzag stitch (a setting of 4 to 5 for stitch width and 1 for stitch length) for everything unless otherwise noted. If a medium zigzag is noted, use a setting of 3 to 4 for stitch width and 1 or a little less for stitch length. You can also use satin stitch. To avoid using the word zigzag over and over, I sometimes use the word sew, but it means zigzag *unless otherwise noted*.

❋ Sew the pieces with the backing sides together or side by side unless otherwise stated.

❋ Zigzag the pieces side by side whenever possible with no space in between, catching the edges of both pieces as the sewing needle goes back and forth. This makes bending the pieces much easier.

❋ "Reattach" always means with zigzag.

❋ When sewing corners and shapes together, pretend that they are a piece of paper, and crush the pieces down to make it easier to line up the edges.

❋ Some of the handles and curled shapes may seem too small to sew with the sewing machine. I give alternate directions for those pieces.

❋ When sewing shelves on the furniture and other pieces that can't be sewn side by side, always sew on the very edge of the pieces, so the needle lands just off of the fabrics on the outer edge and goes through both thicknesses on the inner edge.

❋ The fusing shrinks everything a little. The measurements I give allow for the shrinking. I also iron the cut pieces an extra time to make sure all of the edges are fused.

❋ When gluing with the glue gun, it's easiest to glue a small section to tack the pieces in place. Then, glue the rest of the edges.

❋ I use "easy-to-bend" 26-gauge covered floral wire.

Making the Fabric Sandwich

Making the fabric sandwich: You need a piece of fast2fuse (C&T Publishing) and 2 pieces of fabric to make a sandwich. One fabric is the outside of the shape and the other is the backing or inside of the shape. I used Kona Cotton in wheat or cream colors for the backing fabrics.

Sandwich the fast2fuse between the 2 fabrics. Follow the manufacturer's directions for fusing. The wrong side of the fabric should be touching the fast2fuse, so the right sides of the fabric show once you fuse everything together.

I usually cut the fast2fuse about ⅛″ (3mm) smaller than the fabrics on each edge just to make sure the iron doesn't touch the fast2fuse.

Fabrics

I use 100% cotton fabric. Cotton can be ironed at the highest temperature which makes it easier to make the fabric sandwich. I always buy the prints that appeal to me the most. I prefer to work with the highest quality fabrics.

Fast2Fuse

Fast2fuse (C&T Publishing) is a heavyweight stabilizer that is fusible on both sides and comes in several weights. Other stabilizers have tiny droplets of glue on the surface that show through the fabric once it is fused. Fast2fuse does not have the droplets; it's smooth and yields a smooth fabric sandwich. That's what makes it my favorite. It comes in several pre-cut sizes as well as by the bolt.

Paints

I have very specific paints that I like to use, but as with everything else, I suggest that you use whatever appeals to you most. I almost always use metallics. For these projects, you can use fabric or acrylic paints. Fabric paints are more flexible on fabric, but acrylics work just as well.

Here are my favorites:

Jacquard Lumiere—gorgeous metallic colors for fabric

Pebeo Setacolor shimmer opaque—gorgeous metallic colors for fabric

FolkArt Color Shift—metallic acrylic colors

Tulip Soft Fabric Paint—I use these for painting faces only.

Tulip Glitter Dimensional Fabric Paint—I brush on Crystal Sparkles for sparkle.

Tulip Metallics Dimensional Fabric Paint—I use the gold for embellishing when I want a raised surface.

For painting faces and figures you will also need the following:

brushes, water container, paper towels, palette, Sakura Pigma Micron fabric markers (size 0.5mm) for the eyes and nose

Painting Tips

Painting the Details

I'll admit that I feel a little intimidated by a blank surface. The best way to develop confidence is to practice on a scrap piece of fabric similar to or the same as the surface you are planning to paint.

Tip ✑
You can definitely get away with using eyes only or eyes and cheeks only. This gives a primitive look that I really like.

For eyes, use a Sakura Pigma Micron fabric marker (size 0.5mm) and make 2 dots close together.

The nose always makes me nervous but ends up looking great every time. I basically draw a long U shape that narrows slightly at the top near the eyes.

The mouth can be made using a very thin brush or fabric markers. I make mine in two downward strokes that meet at the bottom to form a heart shape.

The cheeks can be done a couple of ways: either by putting a little pink paint onto a dry brush, dabbing most of the paint off on a paper towel, and then gently brushing in a circular motion to get a soft circle or by putting a tiny drop of water onto the cheek area, then taking a tiny dot of pink paint and putting it in the middle of the water. With a clean brush, swirl the paint around to blend it inside the water dot.

The fairy doors are easy to paint. I suggest you practice on a scrap. You can paint them all one color, or if you want the planks to show, you can use white and the door color. Put a line of white down first, then use the door color and brush it next to the white and gently stroke back and forth to blend the white into the door color. This gives it the gradation.

You can also use colored pencils or markers and draw the door, then copy it onto printable fabric or paper, and mount it with Fabri-Tac glue. Any method works great.

Basic Supplies

- Any sewing machine with straight and zigzag stitches
- Iron and ironing board
- Sewing needles
- Pins
- Thread (I prefer Gutermann brand in white; feel free to match the thread to the fabric.)
- Small and large scissors
- Cutting mat or surface
- Hot glue gun and glue sticks (I prefer Gorilla brand glue sticks.)
- Permanent fabric glue (I prefer Fabri-Tac by Beacon.)
- Ruler
- Pencil
- Lightweight poster board or card-stock for patterns (optional)

Additional Supplies

- Paints, brushes, water container, paper towels, palette
- Sakura Pigma Micron fabric markers (size 0.5mm) for the eyes and nose
- Embellishments like Swarovski crystal flat-back beads, yarn for hair, vintage stamens, vintage mushrooms, moss, glitter (ArtGlitter)
- Polyester fiberfill (I use Poly-Fil.)
- Inspiration
- Patience

Resources

32 Degrees North
This is my favorite place to get stamens, mushrooms, and other embellishments. They ship very fast, and the products are enchanting.

Etsy
I buy almost all of my fabric, as well as some embellishments, here.

Collapsible Portable Dollhouse

Finished size: approximately 7½″ × 7½″ × 13″ ❧ *Refer to Getting Started (pages 7–11).*

Original

Sew Side A to Side B.

This is a great little house to bring along on a trip. It collapses to fit into a suitcase and sets up in just a few seconds.

You can also use some of the Fairy Furniture (page 18) in this house.

What You Need

* Basic Supplies, page 11.

* 5 pieces 15″ × 18″ (38.1 × 45.7cm) medium-weight fast2fuse (C&T Publishing)

* 2 pieces 9″ × 16″ (22.9 × 40.6cm) fabric for house

* 2 pieces 9″ × 16″ (22.9 × 40.6cm) fabric for house backing

* 2 pieces 9″ × 9″ (22.9 × 22.9cm) fabric for house base

* 1 piece 15″ × 18″ (38.1 × 45.7cm) fabric for roof

* 1 piece 15″ × 18″ (38.1 × 45.7cm) fabric for roof backing

* 2 pieces 11″ × 17″ (27.9 × 43.2cm) fine-print, monochromatic fabric for divider

* 2 small buttons ¼″ (6mm)

* 4″ (10.2cm) of ⅛″-wide (3mm) elastic

* Embellishments

* **Paints**

Painted house

Instructions

1. Cut 2 pieces 9″ × 16″ (22.9 × 40.6cm) of fast2fuse and use the house and house backing fabrics to make 2 fabric sandwiches (see Making a Fabric Sandwich, page 9). *fig A*

2. Trace the house pattern piece (page 17) onto the fabric sandwiches and cut them out. Mark the doors and cut them out. Paint the backside of the doors and let them dry.

3. Zigzag around the doors and the door opening. Reattach the doors at the sides (backstitching at both ends), so they can open and close.

4. Sew the house sections together side by side. *fig B*

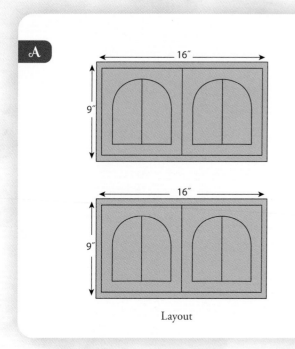

A

Layout

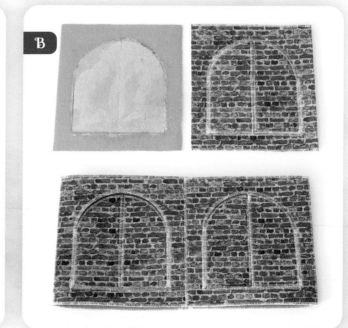

B

5. Cut 1 piece 9″ × 9″ (22.9 × 22.9cm) of fast2fuse and use the base fabrics to make a fabric sandwich.

6. Mark the base pattern piece (page 17) onto the fabric sandwich and cut it out. Cut the base on the lines diagonally from corner to corner to make 4 triangular pieces. Mark the outer edges. *fig C*

7. Zigzag around the triangles. Sew the outer edge of the base triangles to the bottom edges of the house pieces. *fig D*

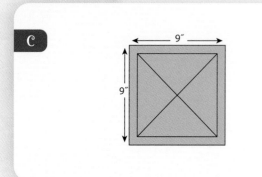

C

D

8. Cut 1 piece 15″ × 18″ (38.1 × 45.7cm) of fast2fuse and use the roof and roof backing fabrics to make a fabric sandwich.

9. Mark the roof pattern pieces (page 17) onto the sandwich and cut them out. Mark the bottom edges. Zigzag the roof pieces together only at the sides, leaving the last seam open. *fig E*

10. Sew the bottom edge of 1 roof piece to the top edge of the house piece on the end. *fig F*

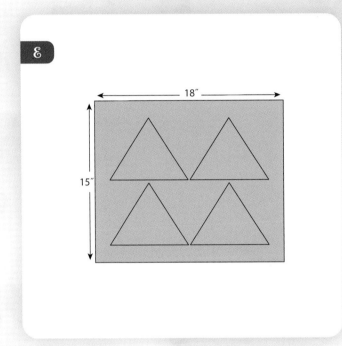

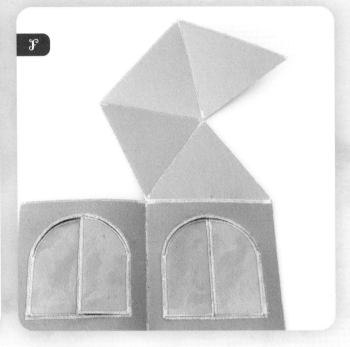

11. Sew the remaining edges of the roof, house, and base pieces all at once. Since they are connected, you can do this by folding the roof and the house pieces in half.

12. Sew the opposite outer edge of the base piece. *fig G*

13. To secure the roof, cut 2 pieces of elastic about 1″ (2.5cm) long and fold them in half. Hand or machine sew the elastic to the 2 unattached roof corners to make loops. Sew 2 tiny buttons onto the corresponding house corners. *fig H*

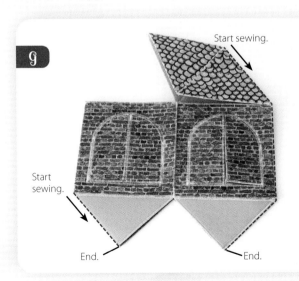

14. Cut 1 piece of fast2fuse 11″ × 17″ (27.9 × 43.2cm) and use the divider fabric to make a fabric sandwich. *fig I*

15. Trace the divider pattern piece (page 17) onto the fabric sandwich and cut it out. Mark the slits. Cut the slits about ⅛″ (3mm) wide down the middle of each divider. Zigzag around both pieces. Join the pieces by sliding the slits together. *fig J*

16. Carefully slip the dividers into the house. The dividers will hold the house nicely in place. *fig K*

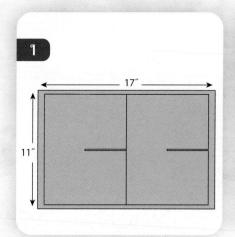

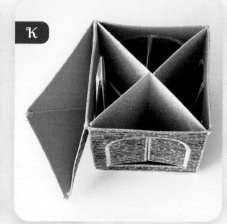

17. Fold the roof over the house and secure it in place with the elastic and buttons.

18. To make a platform, so the furniture can sit higher inside the house, use the leftover fabric sandwich pieces. Cut 4 triangular shapes using the base pattern as a guide. Cut the triangles ¼″ (6mm) smaller on all three sides. Cut 1″ (2.5cm)-wide strips × the length of the triangle sides. Zigzag a strip to each side of the triangles, sewing the pieces side by side. Fold the sides down and slip the platform into the house. *fig L*

Note ☞

One of the best ways to decorate the house is to paint over the fabric with beautiful metallic paints. I painted the doors, some parts of the roof, and the corners of the house. I love the way the fabric prints show through the paint. Since the decorations need to be relatively flat, you can use glass beads and decorative trims. I used beads, flat velvet leaves, and trims. I sewed elastic loops onto the inside of the door openings and threaded tulle through the loops to make curtains.

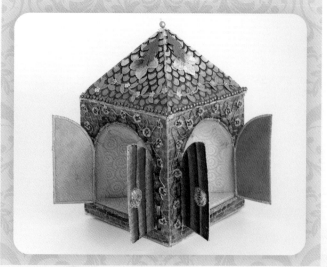

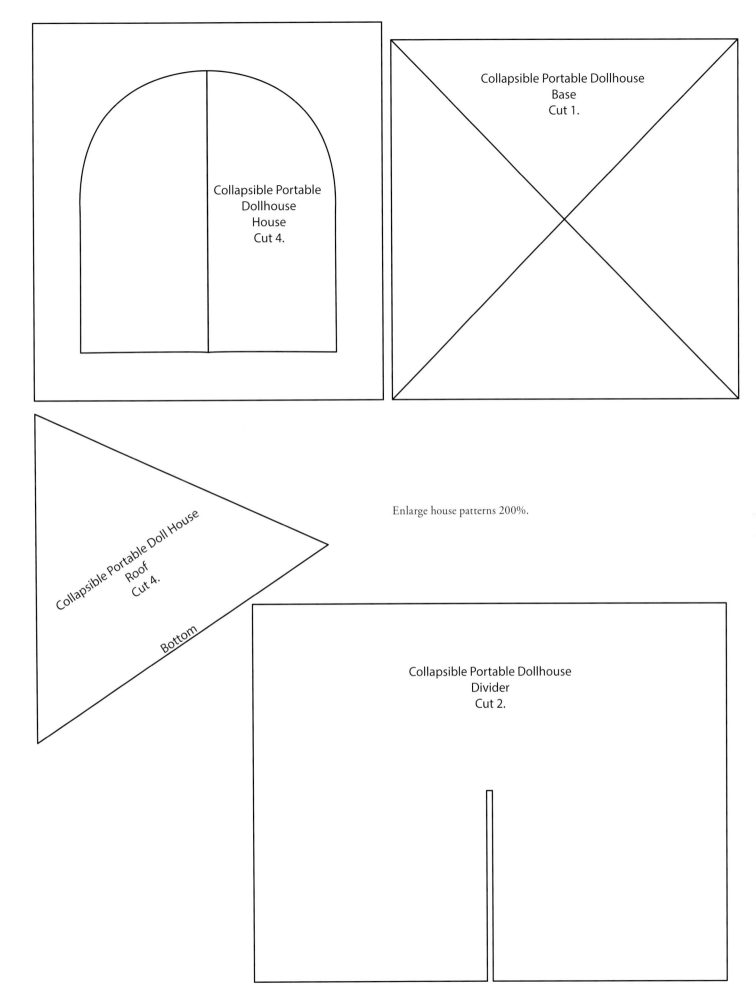

Collapsible Portable
Dollhouse
House
Cut 4.

Collapsible Portable Dollhouse
Base
Cut 1.

Collapsible Portable Doll House
Roof
Cut 4.

Bottom

Enlarge house patterns 200%.

Collapsible Portable Dollhouse
Divider
Cut 2.

Fairy Furniture

What You Need

Note

These are the basic supplies needed to make most of the furniture. Some of the pieces need other supplies. These extra supplies are listed with each project.

❀ Basic Supplies, page 11.

❀ 1 piece 15″ × 18″ (38.1 × 45.7cm) medium-weight fast2fuse (C&T Publishing)

❀ 15″ × 18″ (38.1 × 45.7cm) or 1 fat quarter (45.7 × 55.9cm) total of delicate-print fabrics for furniture

❀ 15″ × 18″ (38.1 × 45.7cm) or 1 fat quarter (45.7 × 55.9cm) fabric for furniture backing

❀ Embellishments

The furniture is really fun to make even though at first it may seem daunting. I always think it's going to be really difficult, but it comes together easily, and it looks so cute when it's done. The irregularity of the finished pieces is what makes them so charming. I usually make one large fabric sandwich (see Making a Fabric Sandwich, page 9) with cotton fabric on one side and a delicate print on the other side. That will yield many pieces of furniture. In my samples, I used several prints I liked and painted the backing fabric gold for some of the furniture.

For the decorations inside the furniture, I use anything that I think looks cute; like shells or acorns, and vintage stamens and mushrooms. Although all of the furniture will not fit into the Collapsible Portable Dollhouse (page 12) or the Teapot (page 50), some of the pieces will fit inside, and it's fun to let the others spill out and around the houses.

Although the furniture shapes are different, the instructions for many of the pieces are very similar. The drawers all get constructed the same way, shelves are attached the same way, corners all get sewn the same way, etc.

Before You Start

Before proceeding, make a fabric sandwich using the fast2fuse and the furniture and furniture backing fabrics (see Making a Fabric Sandwich, page 9).

Bathtub

Finished size: approximately 1¾″ × 1¼″ × 2½″   *Refer to Getting Started (pages 7–11).*

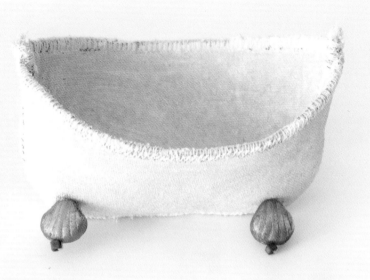

Additional Supplies

❋ **Fabric paint**

❋ **4 beads for tub feet**

❋ **Fabri-Tac glue**

Instructions

1. Trace 2 tub pattern pieces (below) onto the fabric sandwich and cut them out. *fig A*

2. Sew the shapes together at the bottom edge. Zigzag the top edge. *fig B*

3. Sew the sides together, and make sure to backstitch at both ends. *fig C*

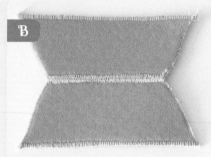

4. Turn the tub inside out to give it a nice rounded shape. *fig D*

5. Paint the tub and let it dry.

6. Glue on beads for feet; I used shell beads that look like a clawfoot.

Fairy Furniture
Bathtub
Cut 1.

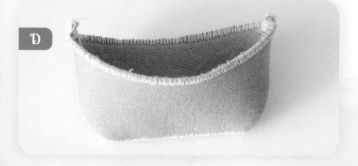

❧ Sink ❧

Finished size: approximately 1½″ × 3¾″ × 2¾″ ❧ *Refer to Getting Started (pages 7–11).*

Additional Supplies

✳ **Tiny crystals to decorate mirror**

✳ **2 beads for knobs**

✳ **Fabric paint**

✳ **Silver duct tape or foil**

✳ **Dimensional paint for the mirror**

Instructions

1. Trace the sink patterns pieces (page 22) onto the fabric sandwich and cut them out. Mark the lines separating the sections on the wall/floor piece. *fig A*

2. Cut the wall/floor shape on the line to separate the sections. Reattach the sections using a zigzag stitch. Zigzag around the whole wall/floor shape.

3. Using tiny scissors, cut the circle in the middle of the sink *leaving it attached at the top edge of the sink.* Zigzag the inner and outer edges of the circle. If it seems too hard to sew the inner circle, just skip it.

4. Make the mirror by tracing the oval shape onto silver duct tape or foil. Cut the oval a little smaller than your outline, and glue it on. *fig B*

A

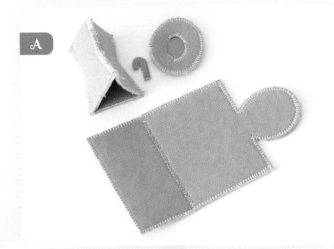

B

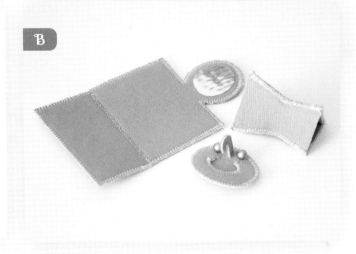

5. Sew the 3 sink base pieces together, crushing them down as you stitch, so you can line up the edges.

6. Sew beads onto the sink for knobs. Glue the faucet in place.

7. Glue the sink onto the narrower end of the base piece. Fold the wall/floor piece, so it stands up. This will be the wall and floor behind and under the sink. *fig C*

8. Paint the sink, the background wall/floor piece, and the faucet. I used dimensional paint and Swarovski crystals to decorate the mirror.

9. Glue the sink base to the floor section.

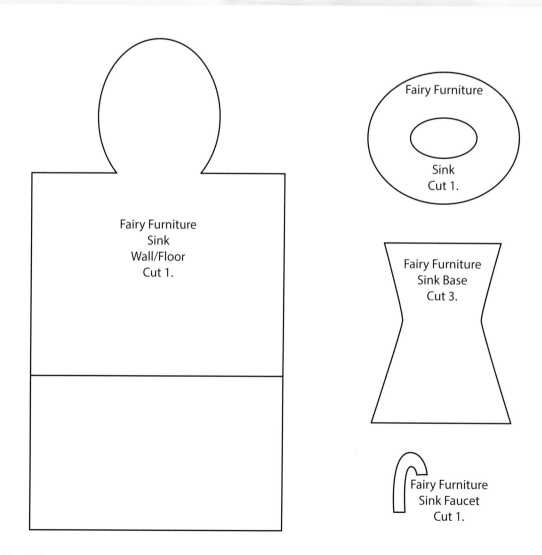

Fairy Furniture
Sink
Wall/Floor
Cut 1.

Fairy Furniture

Sink
Cut 1.

Fairy Furniture
Sink Base
Cut 3.

Fairy Furniture
Sink Faucet
Cut 1.

❧ Toilet ❧

Finished size: approximately 2″ × 2¾″ × 3″ ❧ *Refer to Getting Started (pages 7–11).*

Additional Supplies

❋ 1 bead for the handle

❋ Fabri-Tac glue

❋ Fabric or acrylic paints

Instructions

1. Trace the toilet pattern pieces (page 24) onto the sandwich and cut them out. Mark the lines separating the wall/floor shape.

2. Cut the wall/floor shape on the lines to separate the sections. Reattach the sections with a zigzag stitch. Zigzag around the whole wall/floor shape.

3. Using tiny scissors, cut the circle in the toilet. Zigzag the inner and outer edges of the toilet seat and the cover. If it seems too hard to sew the inner edge, just skip it.

4. Sew the 3 toilet base pieces together, crushing them down so you can line up the edges. *fig A*

5. Sew the corners on the toilet tank, and sew the bead on for the handle. *fig B*

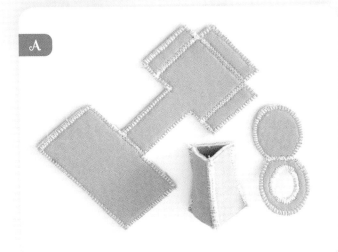

A

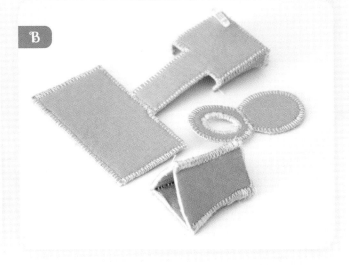

B

6. Glue the toilet piece to the base piece. *fig C*

7. Glue the toilet base to the floor section. Bend the toilet tank up, and glue the seat cover to the tank. *fig D*

8. Paint the toilet, tank, and floor.

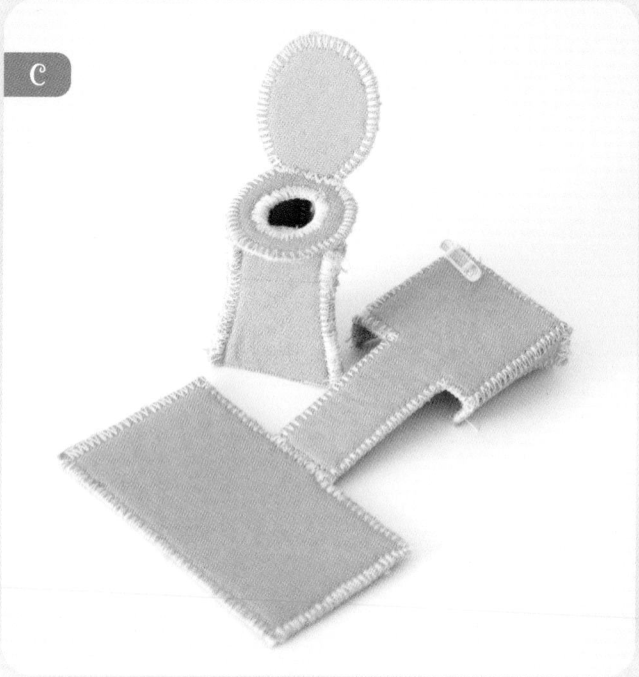
C

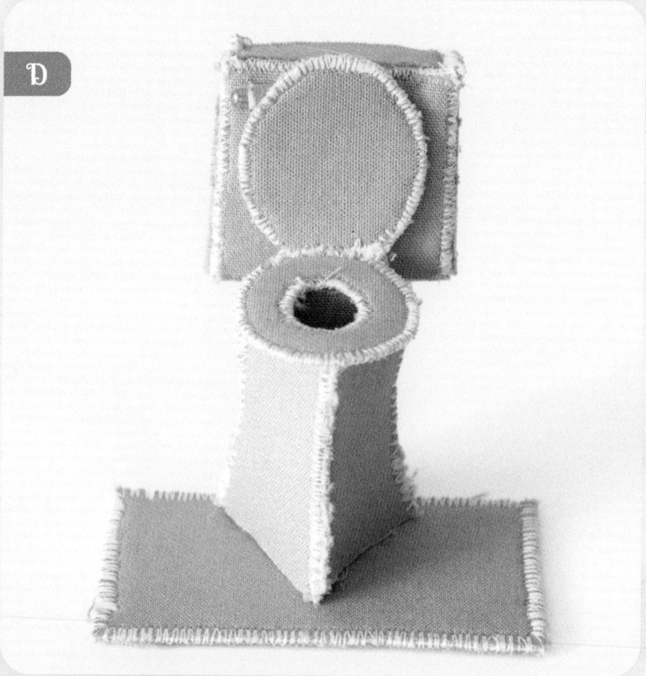
D

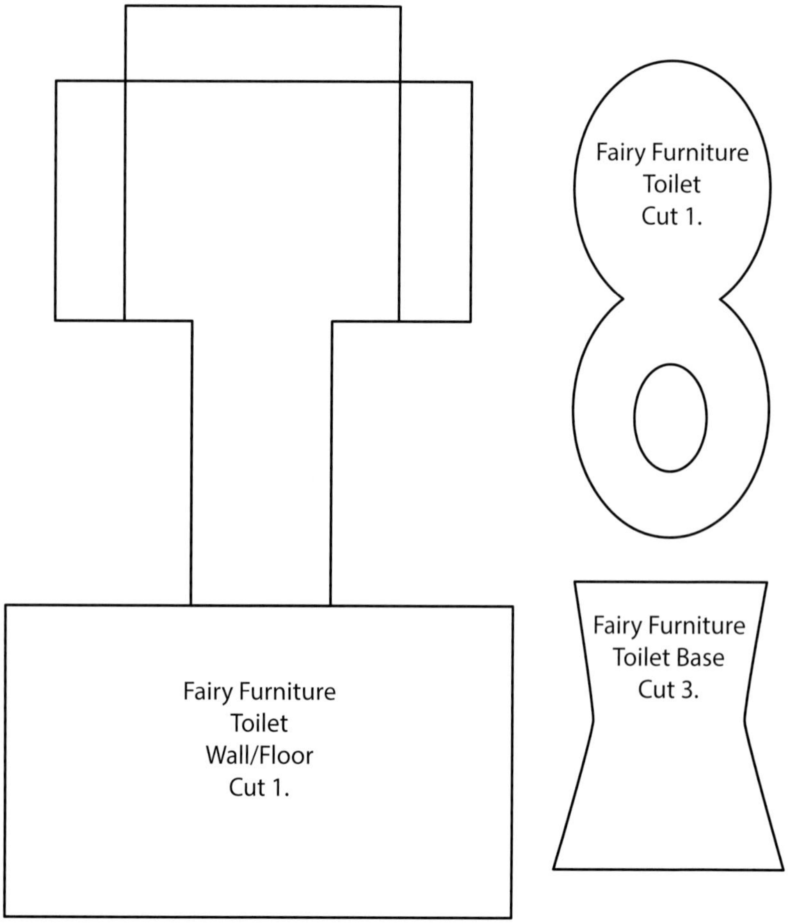
Fairy Furniture
Toilet
Wall/Floor
Cut 1.
Fairy Furniture
Toilet
Cut 1.
Fairy Furniture
Toilet Base
Cut 3.

TOILET PAPER ROLL

Additional Supplies

- **Easy-to-bend floral wire**
- **Small wooden shape or spool**
- **Tiny strip of paper or painted fabric**

To make the toilet paper holder, use a tiny wooden spool or another shape that has a hole in the top for the base. Make the toilet paper out of a narrow strip of paper or painted fabric that has been rolled up into a tiny roll. Put floral wire through the roll, and bend it in half, shaping it to accommodate the roll. Glue the wire into the hole in the base.

～∾ Armoire ∾～

Finished size: approximately 1″ × 4½″ × 2¾″   ✿   *Refer to Getting Started (pages 7–11).*

Additional Supplies

✳ 3 beads for knobs

✳ Thick floral wire
   for clothes rod
   (optional)

✳ Embellishments

Instructions

1. Trace the armoire and drawer pattern pieces (page 27) onto the fabric sandwich and cut them out. Mark the lines separating the sections. Mark the doors and the placement for the drawer.

2. Cut on the lines to separate the sections for the armoire and the drawer. Cut out the doors and the opening for the drawer. *fig A*

3. Zigzag around the doors and the opening for the door and drawer. Reattach the doors at the sides, so they can swing open. Reattach the side, back, top, and bottom sections of the armoire. Reattach the sides of the drawer and zigzag around the outer edge of the drawer. *fig B*

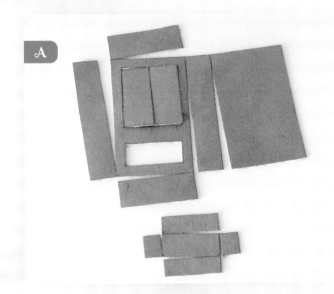

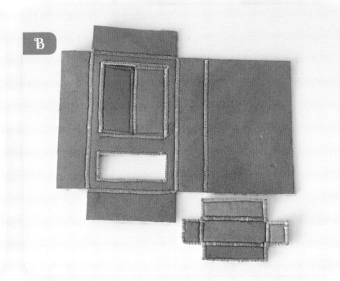

4. Sew the corners of the armoire and the drawer. Fold the pieces as if they were a piece of paper, crushing them down, so you can line up the edges. *fig C*

5. Hand sew or glue the back of the armoire. Sew beads onto the doors and drawer to make the knobs. *fig D*

6. To add a bar to hang the clothes, cut a piece of floral wire about 3¾″ (9.5cm) long. Bend the ends over, so the length of the bar is slightly longer than the width of the armoire, about 2¾″ (7cm). Push into position, and it will stay in place. You can also add glue to secure it. *fig E*

Fairy Furniture
Armoire
Cut 1.

Fairy Furniture
Armoire Drawer
Cut 1.

⤙ Bookcase ⤚

Finished size: approximately 1″ × 4½″ × 3″   ⚘   *Refer to Getting Started (pages 7–11).*

Additional Supplies

❋ 2 beads for knobs

❋ Embellishments for the inside

Instructions

1. Trace the bookcase and shelf pattern pieces (page 30) onto the fabric sandwich and cut them out. Mark the lines separating the sections and placement for the shelves.

2. Cut the slits in the shelves. Cut on the lines to separate the sections and cut out the doors. *fig A*

3. Zigzag around the shelf pieces and cut the slits open. Zigzag around the doors and the openings for the doors. Reattach the sides, top, and bottom of the bookcase. Reattach the doors at the top of the openings and zigzag around the outer edge of the bookcase. *fig B*

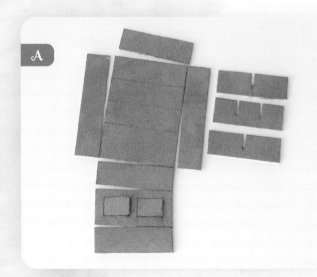

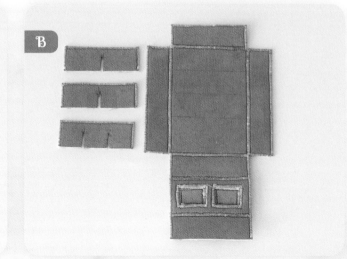

4. Attach the shelves with the slits facing out on the marked lines using a zigzag; sew just catching the edge of the shelf. As you sew, the needle should land just off the outer edge and go through the shelf piece on the inner edge.

5. Fold the bottom of the bookcase up and over to the third line and attach it the same way you attached the shelf divider. This creates the bottom section of the bookcase with two cabinets. *fig C*

6. Sew the top corners of the bookcase. Crush down the shape to match up the edges. Sew the cabinet section to the sides of the bookcase by hand. *fig D*

7. Slide the shelf divider to match up with the slits in the bookcase shelves. *fig E*

8. Sew beads onto the cabinet doors for knobs. *fig F*

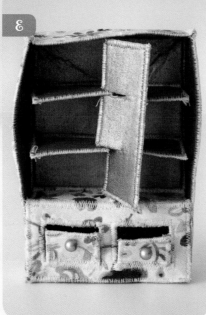

Note ○

Although I like the irregularity of the shelves, you can glue them in place with a tiny drop of hot glue if you want them to be straight.

Fairy Furniture
Bookcase
Divider

Cut 1.

Fairy Furniture
Bookcase
Shelf
Cut 2.

Fairy Furniture
Bookcase
Cut 1.

⊰ Dresser ⊱

Finished size: approximately 1″ × 3″ × 2½″ ✣ *Refer to Getting Started (pages 7–11).*

Additional Supplies

✳ **2 beads for knobs**

Instructions

1. Trace the dresser and drawer pattern pieces (page 32) onto the fabric sandwich and cut them out. Mark the placement for the drawers and the lines separating the sections.

2. Cut on the lines to separate the sections. Cut out the openings for the drawers. *fig A*

3. Zigzag around the openings for the drawers. Reattach the sides, top, bottom, and back of the dresser. Reattach the sides of the drawers and zigzag around the outer edge of the drawers. *fig B*

A

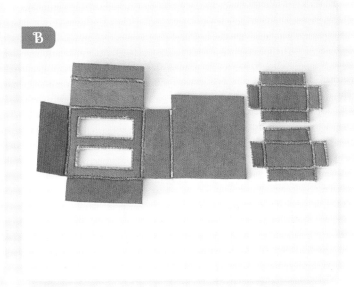

B

4. Sew the corners of the drawers and the dresser. Crush down the shapes, so you can line up the edges. *fig C*

5. Hand sew or glue the back of the dresser.

6. Sew beads onto the drawers to make knobs. *fig D*

Fairy Furniture
Dresser Drawer
Cut 2.

Fairy Furniture
Dresser
Cut 1.

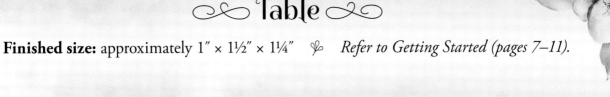

Table

Finished size: approximately 1″ × 1½″ × 1¼″   ✤   *Refer to Getting Started (pages 7–11).*

Instructions

1. Trace the table pattern piece (below) onto the fabric sandwich and cut it out. Mark the lines separating the sections. Cut the sections apart. *fig A*

2. Reattach the sections and zigzag around the whole piece. *fig B*

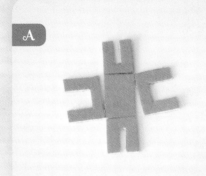

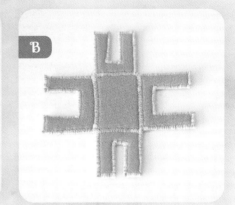

3. Pretend that the table is a piece of paper and fold it diagonally, so you can zigzag the corners together. As you sew, the needle should land just off the fabrics on the outer edge and go through both thicknesses on the inner edge.

4. Open the shape and fold it diagonally to sew the diagonally opposite corners. These may seem harder to do because the first corners are sewn, but just crush it down, so you can line up the edges evenly. *fig C*

5. Open the shape and crease the corners.

Fairy Furniture
Table
Cut 1.

∾ Bed ∾

Finished size: approximately 3″ × 1¾″ × 2″   ✣   *Refer to Getting Started (pages 7–11).*

Additional Supplies

✳ Embellishments

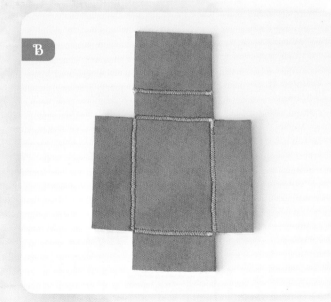

Instructions

1. Trace the bed pattern piece (page 35) onto the fabric sandwich and cut it out. Mark the lines separating the sections. Cut on the lines to separate the sections. *fig A*

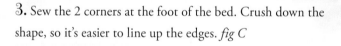

2. Reattach the sections using a zigzag. *fig B*

3. Sew the 2 corners at the foot of the bed. Crush down the shape, so it's easier to line up the edges. *fig C*

4. Fold the back section to make the headboard. Sew the two corners at the head of the bed. Crush down the shape to sew. *figs D–E*

5. Decorate the bed with embellishments.

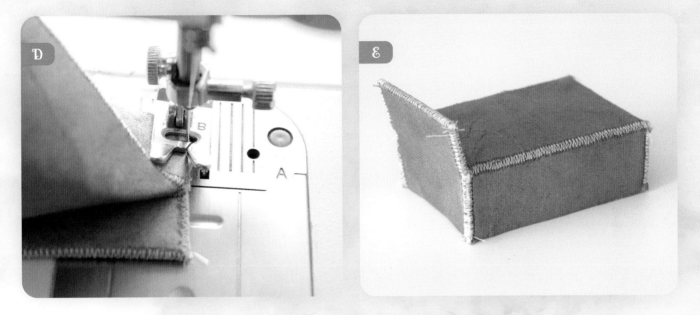

Fairy Furniture
Bed
Cut 1.

❧ Floor Lamp ❧

Finished size: approximately 1½″ × 1½″ × 4″ ❧ *Refer to Getting Started (pages 7–11).*

Additional Supplies

❋ Tiny piece of kraft-tex (C&T Publishing) or other stiff but easy-to-bend material for the shade

❋ Fabri-Tac glue

❋ 6 pieces 6½″ (16.5cm) easy-to-bend floral wire

❋ Ball trim for fringe and pull chain (optional)

I show two options for the lampshade, one made with fabric and with a pull chain and one made with kraft-tex with trim.

Instructions

1. Using the guide for the lamp legs (page 37) or your own design, curl 4 pieces of the floral wire. Use another piece of wire to make the frame for the shade. Bend it according to the guide (page 37) or make your own shape.

2. Trace the shade pattern piece (page 37) onto kraft-tex or other material. *figs A–B*

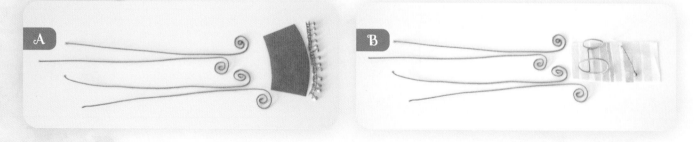

3. Use the remaining piece of wire to tie the legs together. Glue the lampshade onto the wire shade frame, overlapping the ends. *figs C–D*

4. Separate and bend the wire at the top of the legs downward and slide the shade over the top. Make sure the top wires are bent enough so they hold the shade in place. *fig E*

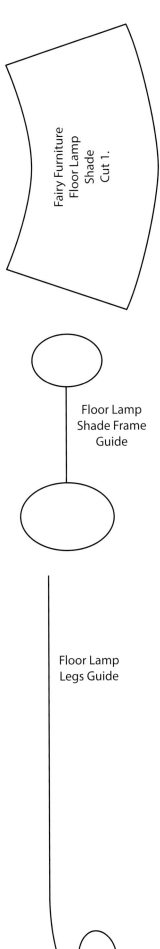

Fairy Furniture
Floor Lamp
Shade
Cut 1.

Floor Lamp
Shade Frame
Guide

Floor Lamp
Legs Guide

❧ Stove ❧

Finished size: approximately 1″ × 2½″ × 2½″   ❧   *Refer to Getting Started (pages 7–11).*

Additional Supplies

* 5 beads for oven knobs
* 2 beads for cabinet handles
* Easy-to-bend floral wire for the stove elements
* Black paint

Instructions

1. Trace the stove and shelf pattern pieces (page 39) onto the fabric sandwich and cut them out. Mark the placement for the shelves, oven door, and cabinet door.

2. Cut on the lines to separate the sections. Cut out the oven and cabinet doors. *fig A*

3. Zigzag around the shelves, openings for the oven door and cabinet, and the doors. Reattach the sides, top, bottom, and back of the stove. Reattach the side edge of the door, so it can swing open. Reattach the oven door at the bottom edge of the opening.

4. Attach the shelves on the lines. *figs B–C*

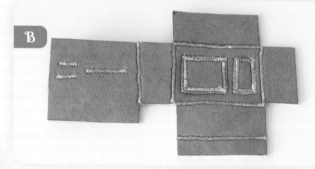

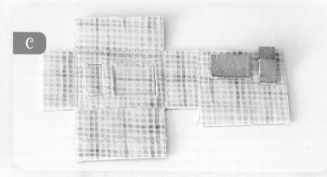

5. Sew the corners of the stove. Crush down the shape so you can line up the edges. *figs D–E*

6. Sew on the beads to make the oven knobs and door handles.

7. Hand sew or glue the back of the stove.

8. To make the stovetop elements use a piece of easy-to-bend floral wire. Using some cutters, pliers, or your hands, coil the wire and paint it black. Glue it onto the stovetop. *fig F*

Fairy Furniture
Stove Shelves
(Optional)

Cut 1.

Cut 2.

Fairy Furniture
Stove
Cut 1.

∽∾ Refrigerator ∾∽

Finished size: approximately 1¼″ × 2¾″ × 4½″   ✺   *Refer to Getting Started (pages 7–11).*

Additional Supplies

❋ **Silver duct tape for the handle**

❋ **Embellishments for the inside**

Instructions

1. Trace the refrigerator and shelf pattern pieces (page 41) onto the fabric sandwich and cut them out. Mark the lines for the shelf placement on the back section and the door on the front section. Measure and cut 1 rectangle 1¼″ × 11″ (3.2 × 27.9cm) for the refrigerator side piece.

2. Cut out the shapes. Cut out the door and cut the slits in the shelves. Cut on the line to separate the bottom section from the front of the fridge.

3. Zigzag around the shelves and clip open the slits. Zigzag around the opening for the door and the door. Reattach the bottom section to the fridge front. Reattach one side edge of the door, so it can swing open. *fig A*

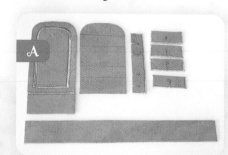

4. Sew the side piece to the front with the pieces side by side. Sew slowly as you go around the curve. The pieces will lift off of the surface of the sewing machine to accommodate the curve. Hold or push the pieces together, so there is no space between them as they go under the presser foot. It will almost feel like you can't do it, but just keep going and you will get to the other side. It will feel clumsy, but in the end, it will look great. *fig B*

5. Sew the shelves onto the back panel on the lines. As you sew, the needle should land just off the outer edge of the shelf piece and go through the piece on the inner edge. Sew the back panel of the refrigerator to the side piece, lining up the bottom. *figs C–D*

6. Crush down the shape and sew the bottom corners of the refrigerator. Pretend that it's a piece of paper and crush it down to line up the edges.

7. Hand sew or glue the back of the refrigerator.

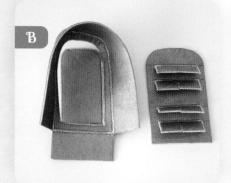

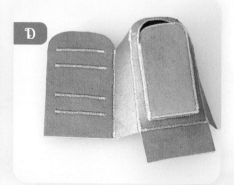

8. Slide the shelf divider to match up with the slits in the shelves. *fig E*

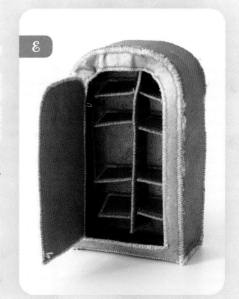

Note ✐

Although I like the irregularity of the shelves, you can glue them in place with a tiny drop of hot glue if you want them to be straight.

9. Make a handle by putting a strip of silver duct tape onto a fabric sandwich scrap. Fill up the fridge with your embellishments.

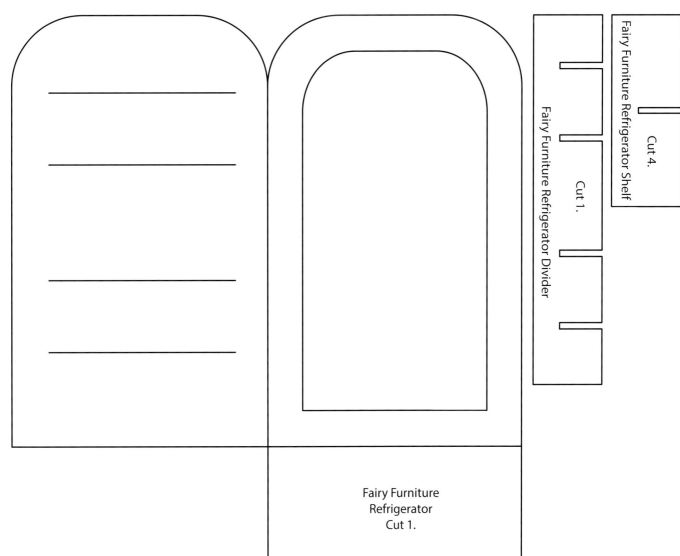

Fairy Furniture Refrigerator Shelf
Cut 4.

Fairy Furniture Refrigerator Divider
Cut 1.

Fairy Furniture
Refrigerator
Cut 1.

Fairy Clothes and Shoes

I'll admit that these fairy clothes and shoes require nimble fingers. They are tiny. The picture shows the size of the clothes and shoes in comparison to a quarter. You can design your own clothes but I give some examples here to get you started. I use kraft-tex which is a cross between paper and fabric.

What You Need

- Basic Supplies, page 11.
- Small piece of kraft-tex (C&T Publishing) or other stiff but easy-to-bend material
- Acrylic paints
- Embellishments
- Floral wire for the hangers

❧ Vest or Dress ❧

Finished size: approximately 1″ × 1½″   ❧   *Refer to Getting Started (pages 7–11).*

Instructions

Note ◡

The pieces are super tiny so they may seem hard to work with at first, but if you just play around with your supplies (tiny flower petals, feathers, stamens, ribbon, tulle, etc.) you will come up with something great and it will get easier to work on the tiny scale.

1. Trace the vest pattern piece (page 45) onto the kraft-tex and cut it out. *fig A*

2. Fold it in half and glue the sides. *fig B*

3. At this point, how you decorate the rest is up to you. Here are some options to consider: paint the vest, add a skirt, add buttons down the front. Or, all of these! *fig C*

Tip ◡

To make tiny hangers, use easy-to-bend floral wire and bend it exactly the same way that a wire coat hanger is constructed.

❧ Shoes ❧

Finished size: approximately ½″ long   ❧   *Refer to Getting Started (pages 7–11).*

The shoes are tiny too. I use kraft-tex again since it's easy to work with. Here I show 3 different examples: a boot, a slide, and a flip-flop. These are so tiny you may have to use tweezers. Decorate the shoes with metallic paints, Swarovski crystals, and other tiny decorations.

Instructions

1. Trace the shoe pattern pieces (below) onto kraft-tex and cut them out.

2. Fold the shapes for the slide and flip-flop and glue the pieces together.

3. Sew the boot pieces together by hand or machine using a straight stitch and a ⅛″ seam allowance. They don't have a sole piece; when they stand up, you can't see it anyway. *figs A–C*

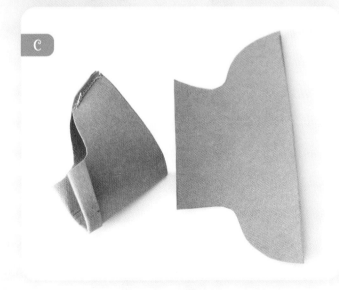

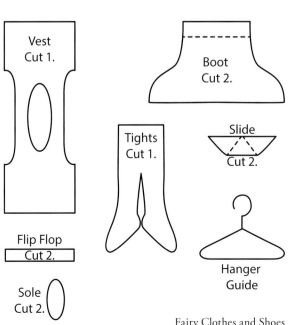

Vest
Cut 1.

Boot
Cut 2.

Tights
Cut 1.

Slide
Cut 2.

Flip Flop
Cut 2.

Sole
Cut 2.

Hanger
Guide

Mushroom Fairy House with Light

Finished size: approximately 4″ × 4″ × 4½″   ✤   *Refer to Getting Started (pages 7–11).*

What You Need

- Basic Supplies, page 11.
- 1 piece 15″ × 18″ (38.1 × 45.7cm) medium-weight fast2fuse (C&T Publishing)
- 2 pieces 9″ × 12″ (22.9 × 30.5cm) white or cream fabric for mushroom and backing
- Fabric or acrylic paints
- LED tea light
- 4″ (10.2cm) diameter cardboard cake round

- Utility knife (I use Exacto.)
- Cutting mat or surface
- 1 piece 8″ × 8″ (20.3 × 20.3cm) of velvet
- Polyester fiberfill (I use Poly-Fil.)
- 3″ (7.6cm) diameter paper doily
- Moss
- Embellishments

Instructions

1. Cut 1 piece of fast2fuse 9″ × 12″ (22.9 × 30.5cm). Using the mushroom fabric, make a fabric sandwich (see Making a Fabric Sandwich, page 9). Trace the mushroom pattern pieces (page 49) onto the sandwich and cut them out.

2. Sew the seams on the mushroom cap and stem using a zigzag. To turn the stem right side out, fold the top edge into the shape and keep pushing in until it's inside out. Turn the cap inside out and zigzag around the outside edge. *figs A–B*

3. Cut the windows in the stem piece. Paint the mushroom cap and the stem. Paint the underside of the cap. If you plan to use this as an ornament, attach a string onto the cap by hand. *fig C*

4. Trace around the tealight in the center of the cake round and the doily. Using a sharp utility knife, cut out the circle on a cutting mat (I poke holes with the tip of the knife to make a perforated line and then poke the circle out). Push the tealight through the hole to make sure it fits through the cake round.

5. Cut the velvet about 1½″ (3.8cm) larger than the cake round all the way around. Hand sew around the outside edge of the circle using ¼″ long running stitches. *fig D*

6. Put the cake round in the center of the velvet and gently pull the stitching to gather the edge of the velvet. Be careful not to break the thread. Knot the thread ends. *fig E*

7. Cut a circle in the top side of the velvet for the tea light. Put a little stuffing under the velvet on the top side, to give it a little fullness. *fig F*

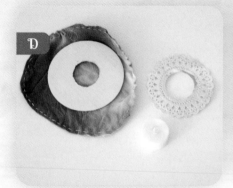

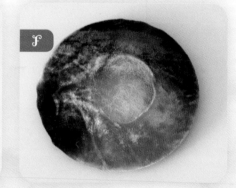

8. Push the stuffing away from the opening and glue the velvet to the edge. *fig G*

9. Place the tealight through the hole and glue around the edge of the tealight with a glue gun. Use as little glue as possible. Put the stem over the tealight; if the stem is too tight, cut a little off the bottom to make the opening bigger. Put a little bit of glue around the bottom edge of the stem. This will be covered with moss, so it's okay if some glue shows. *figs H–I*

10. Glue the doily onto the bottom of the velvet base using a glue gun. The glue comes through the holes in the doily, so it's best to use very little glue and press gently to avoid touching the glue. *fig J*

11. Glue the mushroom cap onto the stem. Make a door from fabric sandwich scraps or kraft-tex. Paint the door (see Painting the Details, page 10).

12. Decorate the house using your embellishments. *fig K*

K

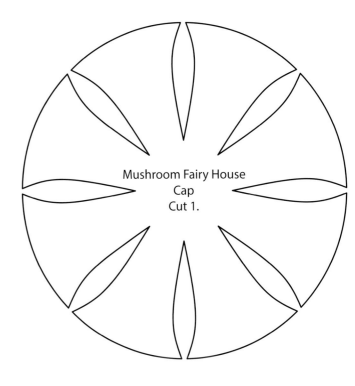

Mushroom Fairy House
Cap
Cut 1.

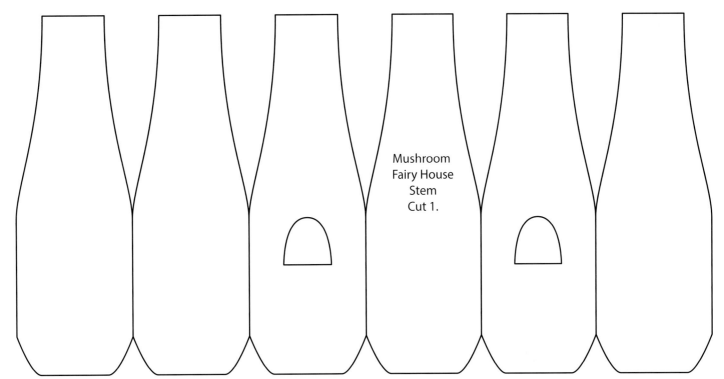

Mushroom
Fairy House
Stem
Cut 1.

Tea Service Fairy Village

⮜⮞ Teapot House ⮜⮞

Finished size: approximately 7½″ × 12″ × 16½″   ❧   *Refer to Getting Started (pages 7–11).*

What You Need

❋ Basic Supplies, page 11.

❋ 4 pieces 15″ × 18″ (38.1 × 45.7cm) medium-weight fast2fuse (C&T Publishing)

❋ 2 pieces 15″ × 18″ (38.1 × 45.7cm) fabric for teapot

❋ 2 pieces 15″ × 18″ (38.1 × 45.7cm) fabric for teapot backing

❋ 1 piece 15″ × 18″ (38.1 × 45.7cm) fabric for curly top

❋ 1 piece 15″ × 18″ (38.1 × 45.7cm) fabric for curly top backing

❋ 2 pieces 12″ × 12″ (30.5 × 30.5cm) fabric for tray

❋ Embellishments

❋ Fabric or acrylic paints

❋ Small piece of kraft-tex (C&T Publishing) for the window boxes (optional)

❋ Polyester fiberfill (I use Poly-Fil.)

Instructions

1. Make 2 fabric sandwiches (see Making the Fabric Sandwich, page 9) using 2 pieces each of fast2fuse and the teapot and teapot backing fabrics. Make 1 fabric sandwich using fast2fuse and the curly top and curly top backing fabrics. Cut 1 piece of fast2fuse 12″ × 12″ (30.5 × 30.5cm) and make a fabric sandwich using the tray fabric and set aside.

Tea Service Fairy Village 51

2. Trace the teapot pattern pieces (pages 66–69) onto the fabric sandwiches and cut them out. Mark the doors (on one section only), and cut them out. Zigzag around the doors and the door opening. Cut out the handles and spout. *fig A*

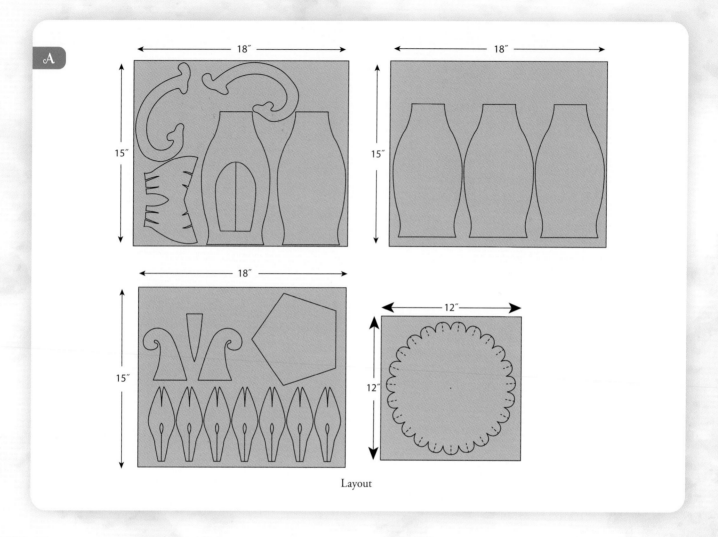

Layout

3. Reattach the doors at the sides, so they swing open. *fig B*

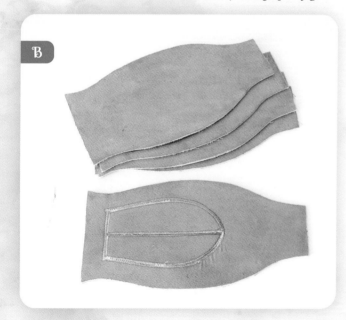

4. Trace the curly top and leafy top pattern pieces (page 66) onto the fabric sandwich and cut. Mark the detail sewing lines on all the pieces. Cut on the dashed lines on the curly top pieces.

> **Note**
> The leaf shapes are a little tricky, but not hard. They require you to sew darts on the wrong side *and* right side of each leaf. Just make sure to read the directions carefully as you go to be sure you are sewing on the correct side.

5. Zigzag around the leaf shapes and the curly top shapes. Sew the slits closed on the curly top pieces.

6. Sew the triangular piece to one of the curly top pieces, lining up the bottom of the shapes. Sew the leaf shapes together at the sides starting at the blunt end and sewing the straight edge up to the start of the curve. *fig C*

7. Sew the slits on the spout to form darts using a medium zigzag. It may feel clumsy as you're doing it, but just keep sewing the darts, crushing the shape down, so you can line up the edges. It will look great when you are done. Sew the handles together on the *outside* edges only. *fig D*

8. Sew the final seams on the spout crushing it down to help line the edges up. Using your hands, open the spout to shape it. *fig E*

9. To shape the leaves, fold each one in half, with *right* sides together. Starting at the point, sew with a medium zigzag to close up the slits. Sew all of the leaves before going to the next step. *fig F*

10. Fold each leaf in half in the other direction, with the *wrong* sides together. Starting at the blunt end, sew along the edge and the curve. *fig G*

11. Sew the final seam of the leaf pieces. *fig H*

12. Sew the teapot sections together, crushing down the shape to make it easier to line up the edges. Keep sewing until the whole teapot is complete.

13. Put your hands inside the shape and push out the edges to open the shape. *fig I*

14. Zigzag the base onto the bottom edges of the teapot by lining up each edge with an edge on the base. You will have to crush down the shape to do that. You can also hand sew the base to the teapot. *fig J*

15. Trace the desired number of window and awning pattern pieces (page 66) onto fabric sandwich scraps and cut them out. Paint the windows and the awnings. Trace the window box pattern pieces (page 66) onto kraft-tex or other stiff material (optional). *fig K*

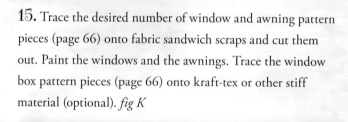

16. Glue the awnings and window boxes to the windows with a glue gun. *fig L*

17. Draw the outlines of the windows onto the teapot wherever you want them to go. Cut out an opening a little smaller than the shape that you drew. Glue the windows onto the house using a glue gun. Decorate the window box with embellishments. *fig M*

18. Sew the remaining seam on the curly top. Go slowly around the curl. If it's too hard to sew the curl, you can hand sew it instead. Stuff the curly top with fiberfill using a marker or pencil. Put the curly top onto the leafy top. *fig N*

19. Put a few pipe cleaners or covered gardening wire into the handle to fatten it up. Make sure to use something thin enough that will allow you to sew the inner edge of the handle closed. Zigzag the handle on the inner edge. *fig O*

20. Mark the desired placement for the handle and spout. Hand sew the handle onto the teapot and glue the spout on. Position the top onto the teapot and glue it on. *fig P*

21. Make a door from fabric sandwich scraps or kraft-tex. Paint the door (see Painting the Details, page 10). Sew on beads to make doorknobs. Make a sign with the name of your house and glue it on.

Sugar and Creamer Carriage House

Finished size: approximately 5½″ × 7½″ × 10″   ❧ *Refer to Getting Started (pages 7–11).*

Note

If the windows are too challenging, you can always omit them.

What You Need

* Basic Supplies, page 11.

* 2 pieces 15″ × 18″ (38.1 × 45.7cm) medium-weight fast2fuse (C&T Publishing)

* 6″ × 18″ (15.2 × 45.7cm) fabric for sugar bowl

* 6″ × 18″ (15.2 × 45.7cm) fabric for sugar bowl backing

* 9″ × 18″ (22.9 × 45.7cm) fabric for creamer

* 9″ × 18″ (22.9 × 45.7cm) fabric for creamer backing

* 2 pieces 8″ × 12″ (20.3 × 30.5cm) fabric for tray

* Moss

* Embellishments

* kraft-tex (C&T Publishing)

Note

Plan on painting the handle pieces since they are only a single layer of the fabric sandwich.

Instructions

Cut the fast2fuse into 3 sizes: 6″ × 18″ (17.8 × 27.9cm) for the sugar bowl, 9″ × 18″ (20.3 × 20.3cm) for the creamer, and 8″ × 12″ (17.8 × 17.8cm) for the oval tray. Using the corresponding size fabrics, make 3 fabric sandwiches (see Making a Fabric Sandwich, page 9). Set aside the piece for the tray. *fig A*

A   Layout

SUGAR BOWL

For this project use a medium-wide zigzag.

1. Trace the sugar bowl pattern pieces (pages 66–68) onto the appropriate fabric sandwich and cut out. *fig A*

2. Zigzag around the leafy top pieces, the curly top pieces, and the handles. If the handles are too challenging to zigzag, you can paint them instead, to make them firmer.

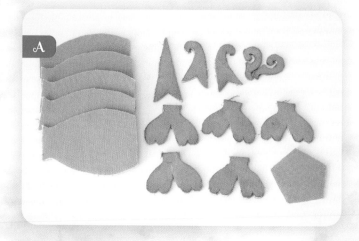

3. Sew the 3 curly top pieces together side by side, lining up the bottom edges. Sew the leafy top pieces together, starting at the blunt end and sewing to the marked dots on the pattern. Sew the sugar bowl pieces, with wrong sides together. *fig B*

4. Sew the final seam on the curly top piece. If it feels too small, you can glue it instead of sewing it. Sew the slits closed on the leafy top pieces. *fig C*

5. Sew the base onto the sugar bowl by hand. It may seem like the base is too big, but if you spread open the bottom edges it will fit together nicely.

6. Trace the smaller window and awning pattern pieces (page 66) onto fabric sandwich scraps and cut them out. Glue the awnings onto the windows.

7. Glue the leafy top onto the curly top. Glue the pieces onto the sugar bowl. Position and mark the handle positions. Hand sew the handles in place. *fig D*

8. Here are suggestions for decorating: Make tiny window boxes for the windows. Use embellishments to decorate them. Glue the windows onto the sugar bowl. Make a door from fabric sandwich scraps or kraft-tex. Paint the door (see Painting the Details, page 10). Use moss and other embellishments to decorate around the door and windows. Make a small sign out of kraft-tex, fabric sandwich scrap, or poster board, with the word "Sugar" on it. *fig E*

CREAMER

For this project use a medium-wide zigzag.

1. Trace the creamer pattern pieces (pages 67–69) onto the appropriate fabric sandwich and cut them out. *fig A*

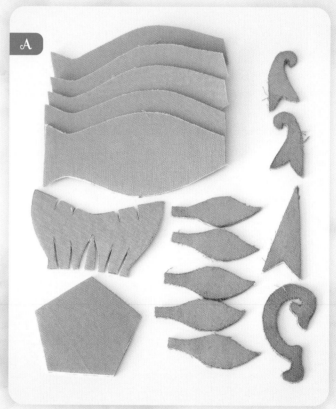

2. Zigzag around the leafy top, curly top, and handle pieces. The handle is a little challenging to zigzag, so you can paint the handle instead, to make it firmer.

3. Sew the 3 curly top pieces together side by side, lining up the bottom edges. Sew the leafy top pieces together starting at the blunt end and sewing halfway down the leaf. *fig B*

4. Sew the creamer pieces with wrong sides together. Sew the base onto the creamer by hand. It may seem like the base is too big but if you spread open the bottom edges, it will fit together nicely. Sew the darts and seams on the spout, as you did on the teapot (see Teapot House, step 7, page 53). *figs C–D*

5. Trace the smaller window and awning pattern pieces (page 66) onto fabric sandwich scraps and cut them out. The cuts in the windows are very small. If they are too challenging to cut out, you can paint the detail onto the window shape. Glue the awnings onto the windows, as you did for the teapot (see Teapot House, steps 15 and 16, pages 54–55). Make tiny window boxes using kraft-tex (optional). *fig E*

6. Sew the final seam on the curly top piece. Glue the leafy top onto the curly top. Glue the pieces onto the creamer. Position and mark the handle position. Hand sew the handles and glue the spout in place. *fig F*

Note
Since the curly top is so tiny, you can glue it together instead of sewing it.

7. Here are suggestions for decorating: Glue the windows onto the creamer. Make a door from fabric sandwich scraps or kraft-tex. Paint the door (see Painting the Details, page 10). Use moss and other embellishments to decorate around the door and windows. Make a small sign out of kraft-tex, a sandwich scrap, or poster board, with the word "Cream" on it.

∾✕∾ Teacup Guest House ∾✕∾

Finished size: approximately 5½″ × 6″ × 5½″   ✎   *Refer to Getting Started (pages 7–11).*

Note ♡
Directions for the saucer are at the end of these instructions.

What You Need

❋ Basic Supplies, page 11.

❋ 1 piece 15″ × 18″ (38.1 × 45.7cm) medium-weight fast2fuse (C&T Publishing)

❋ 2 pieces 7″ × 11″ (17.8 × 27.9cm) fabric for the teacup and handle

❋ 2 pieces 8″ × 8″ (20.3 × 20.3cm) cream fabric for the mushroom

❋ 2 pieces 7″ × 7″ (17.8 × 17.8cm) fabric for the saucer

❋ 4″ (10.2cm) diameter cake round

❋ Moss

❋ Embellishments

Instructions

Cut the fast2fuse into 3 sizes: 7″ × 11″ (17.8 × 27.9cm) for the teacup, 8″ × 8″ (20.3 × 20.3cm) for the mushroom, and 7″ × 7″ (17.8 × 17.8cm) for the saucer. Using the corresponding size fabrics, make 3 fabric sandwiches (see Making a Fabric Sandwich, page 9). Set aside the piece for the saucer. *fig A*

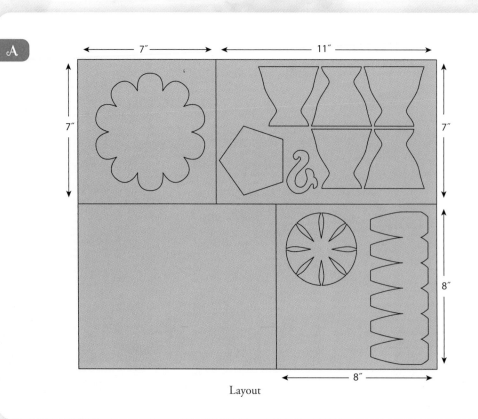

Layout

TEACUP

For this project use a medium-wide zigzag.

1. Trace the teacup pattern pieces (pages 67–68) onto the appropriate fabric sandwich and cut them out.

2. Sew the teacup pieces with wrong sides together. Attach the base onto the cup by hand. Stretch the bottom of the cup to fit the base. Zigzag around the handle piece and sew it onto the cup by hand.

3. Place the cake round into the top of the teacup to open the shape. Glue the round in place with a glue gun.

MUSHROOM

1. Trace the mushroom pattern pieces (pages 68–69) onto the appropriate fabric sandwich and cut them out.

2. Sew and paint the mushroom stem and cap using directions from Mushroom Fairy House with Light (page 46), but note that the stem patterns are different.

3. Cover the cake round with moss. Make a door from fabric sandwich scraps or kraft-tex. Paint the door (see Painting the Details, page 10). Decorate the base of the teacup and around the door.

TRAYS AND SAUCER

The trays and saucer are made in the same way. Sizes for the fabric sandwiches were given with each project.

1. Trace the round tray, oval tray, and saucer pattern pieces (pages 68–69) onto the prepared fabric sandwiches and cut them out. Cut on the dashed lines on each scallop. *fig A*

2. Zigzag around the edge of the shape going around each scallop.

3. Fold each scallop and sew on the cut lines to make a dart in each. This takes a while but it's worth the effort since the darts will shape the tray. *fig B*

A

B

4. Stitch a circle (or oval) using a straight stitch, just inside the scallops to make a slight crease. *fig C*

5. Press each scallop to flatten them out. If you paint your tray, make sure to put parchment on the ironing surface, as well as over the shape.

Note

To make the trays or saucer flatter, you can glue a cardboard oval or a cake round to the bottom, that is the same size as the stitched shape. This will make them more rigid.

C

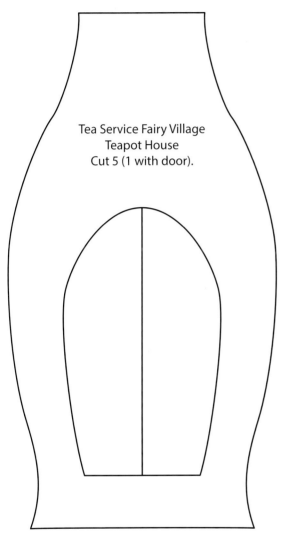

Tea Service Fairy Village
Teapot House
Cut 5 (1 with door).

Enlarge house pattern 200%.

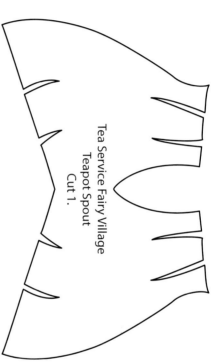

Tea Service Fairy Village
Teapot Spout
Cut 1.

Enlarge spout pattern 200%.

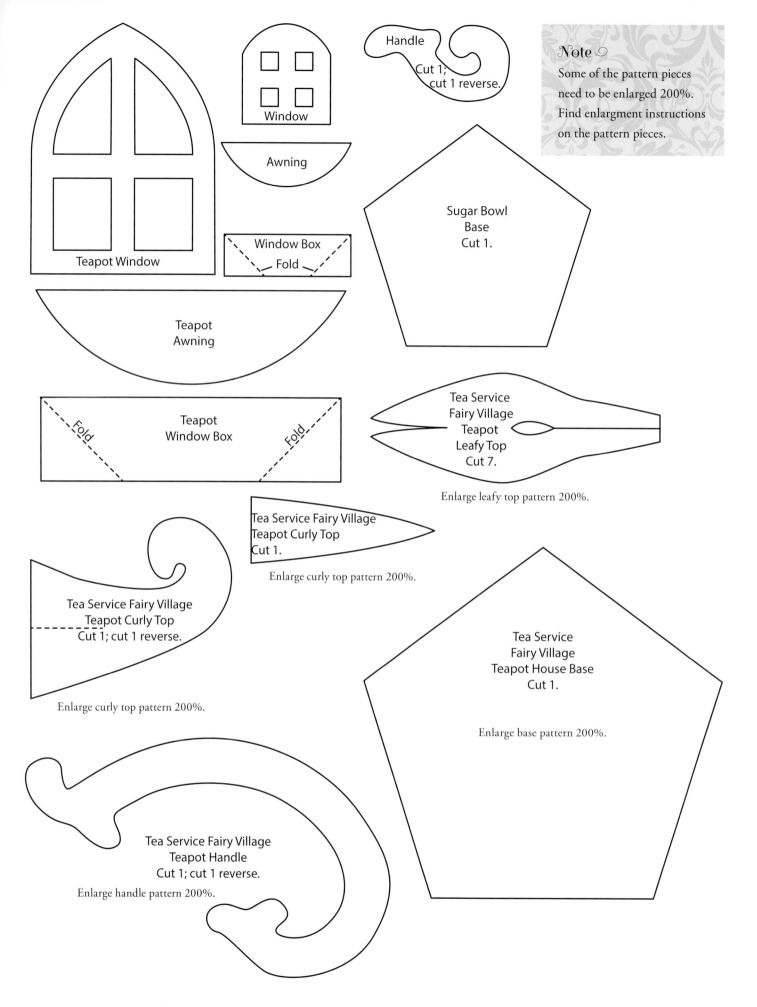

Window

Awning

Handle
Cut 1;
cut 1 reverse.

Teapot Window

Window Box
Fold

Teapot
Awning

Sugar Bowl
Base
Cut 1.

Fold

Teapot
Window Box

Fold

Tea Service
Fairy Village
Teapot
Leafy Top
Cut 7.

Enlarge leafy top pattern 200%.

Tea Service Fairy Village
Teapot Curly Top
Cut 1.

Enlarge curly top pattern 200%.

Tea Service Fairy Village
Teapot Curly Top
Cut 1; cut 1 reverse.

Enlarge curly top pattern 200%.

Tea Service
Fairy Village
Teapot House Base
Cut 1.

Enlarge base pattern 200%.

Tea Service Fairy Village
Teapot Handle
Cut 1; cut 1 reverse.

Enlarge handle pattern 200%.

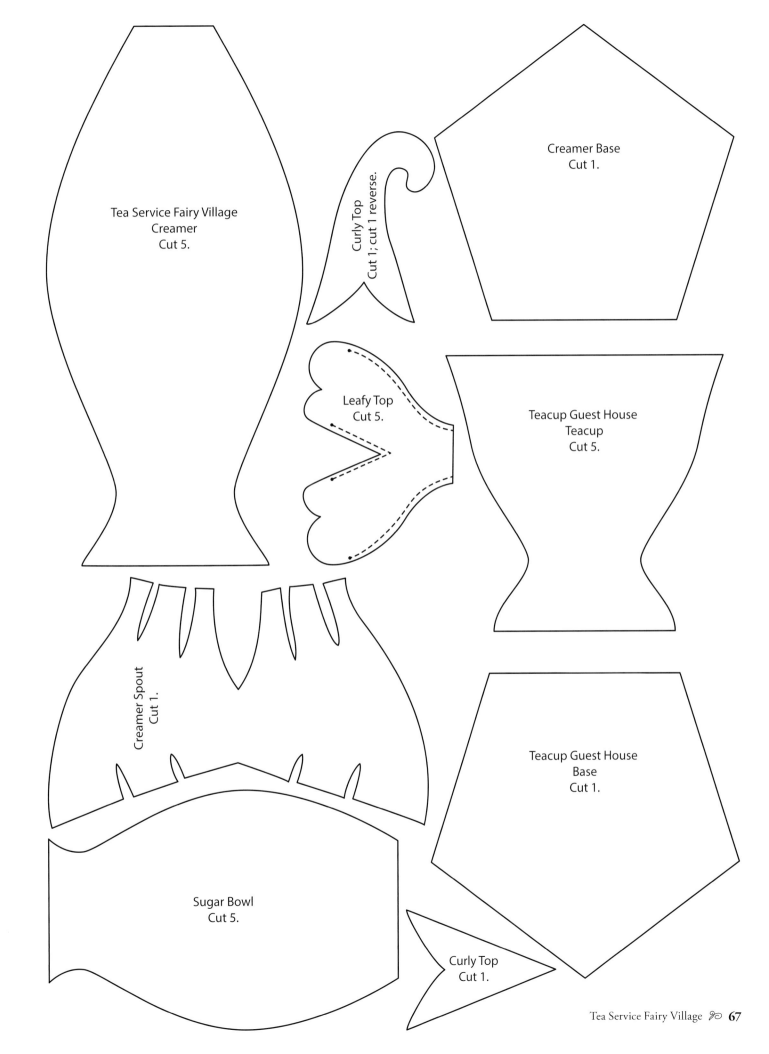

Tea Service Fairy Village
Creamer
Cut 5.

Curly Top
Cut 1; cut 1 reverse.

Creamer Base
Cut 1.

Leafy Top
Cut 5.

Teacup Guest House
Teacup
Cut 5.

Creamer Spout
Cut 1.

Teacup Guest House
Base
Cut 1.

Sugar Bowl
Cut 5.

Curly Top
Cut 1.

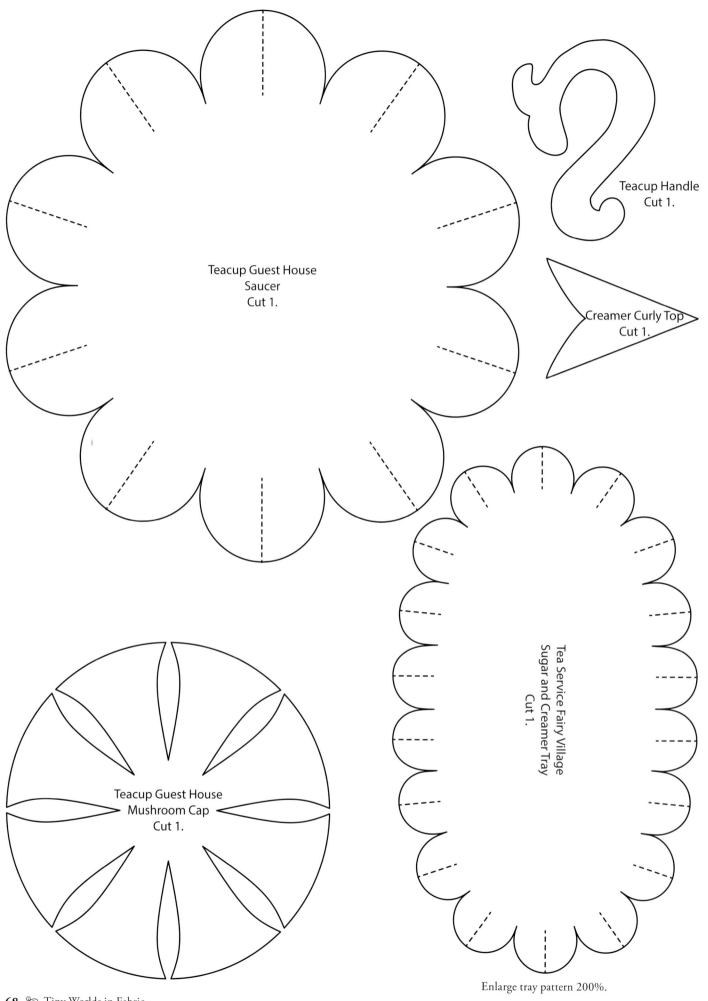

Teacup Handle
Cut 1.

Teacup Guest House
Saucer
Cut 1.

Creamer Curly Top
Cut 1.

Tea Service Fairy Village
Sugar and Creamer Tray
Cut 1.

Teacup Guest House
Mushroom Cap
Cut 1.

Enlarge tray pattern 200%.

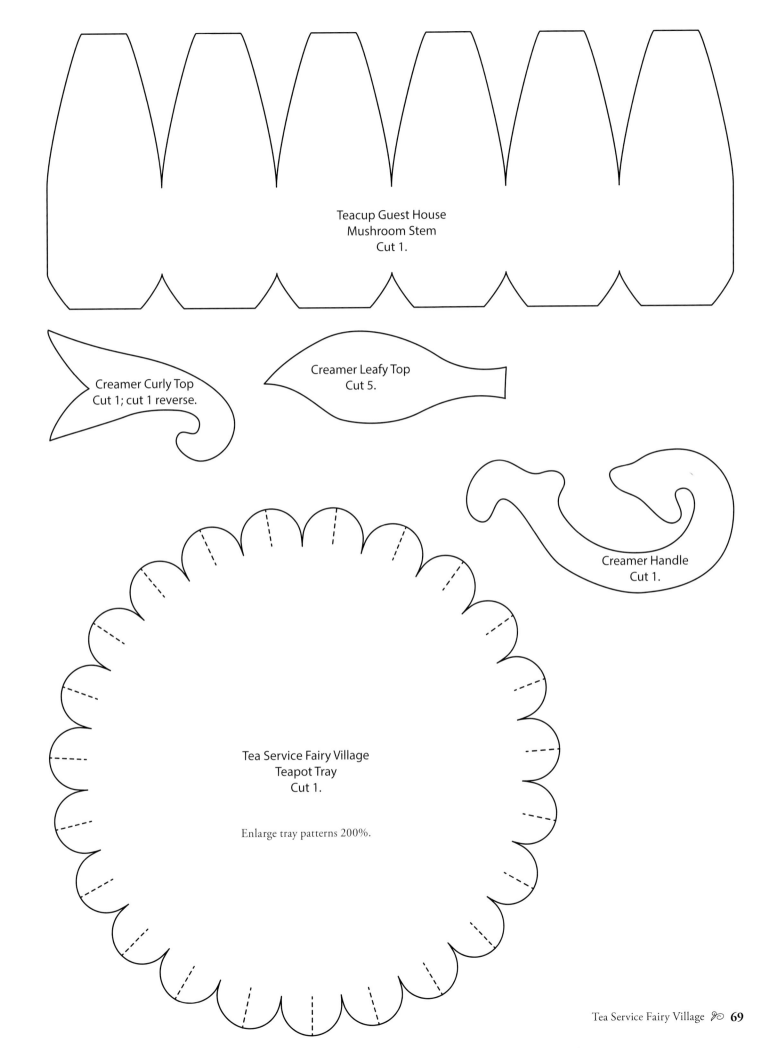

Teacup Guest House
Mushroom Stem
Cut 1.

Creamer Curly Top
Cut 1; cut 1 reverse.

Creamer Leafy Top
Cut 5.

Creamer Handle
Cut 1.

Tea Service Fairy Village
Teapot Tray
Cut 1.

Enlarge tray patterns 200%.

Mermaid Bride and Groom Cake Topper

Finished size: approximately 4″ × 6¼″ × 5″   ✣   *Refer to Getting Started (pages 7–11).*

What You Need

* Basic Supplies, page 11.

* 1 piece 10″ × 10″ (25.4 × 25.4cm) medium-weight fast2fuse (C&T Publishing)

* 2 pieces 10″ × 10″ (25.4 × 25.4cm) fabric for the shell

* 1 piece 9″ × 14″ (22.9 × 35.6cm) flesh-colored fabric for the mermaids

* Polyester fiberfill (I use Poly-Fil.)

* Fabric or acrylic paints

* Fine-point fabric markers

* Glitter and glitter glue (optional)

* Yarn for hair

* Embellishments

* 6″ diameter cardboard cake round (optional)

Instructions

Shells

1. Make a fabric sandwich using the fast2fuse and the shell fabric pieces (see Making a Fabric Sandwich, page 9).

2. Trace the shell pattern piece (page 73) onto the fabric sandwich and mark the sewing lines. Cut out the shells. *fig A*

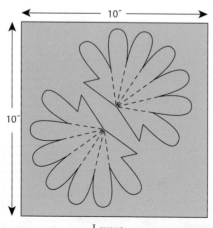

Layout

A

3. Zigzag around the shells. Fold each shell piece on the dashed lines and zigzag on the lines, one at a time, until the whole shell is done. This will shape the shells nicely. *figs B–C*

4. Sew the bottom edges of the shells together.

5. Paint the shells and let them dry thoroughly. *fig D*

Bride and Groom

1. Fold the piece of flesh-colored fabric in half with right sides together. Trace the bride and groom pattern piece (page 73) onto the fabric. Sew on the line using a small straight stitch. Trim about ⅛″ (3mm) from the stitching. Clip the curves making sure not to cut into the seam. *fig E*

2. Cut a 1″ (25mm) slit through one layer of the fabric between the mermaids. Turn right side out. I use a bamboo skewer to push out the tail and the arms. Try not to poke through the stitching. *fig F*

3. Stuff the bride and groom. Start with the tails and arms. Topstitch some detailing on the bride's tail (optional). Continue stuffing the whole shape. Hand sew the opening closed. Sew a line of stitching through the middle to separate the mermaids. *fig G*

4. Paint the mermaids using fabric or acrylic paints. Use a fine-point fabric marker to add eyes to both and a bow tie on the groom. Add cheeks and lips, and glue on the hair. Use glitter glue to add glitter to the figures (optional). *fig H*

5. Glue the mermaids inside the shell using a glue gun and embellish the base. I used a 6″ (15.2cm) cardboard cake round for the base.

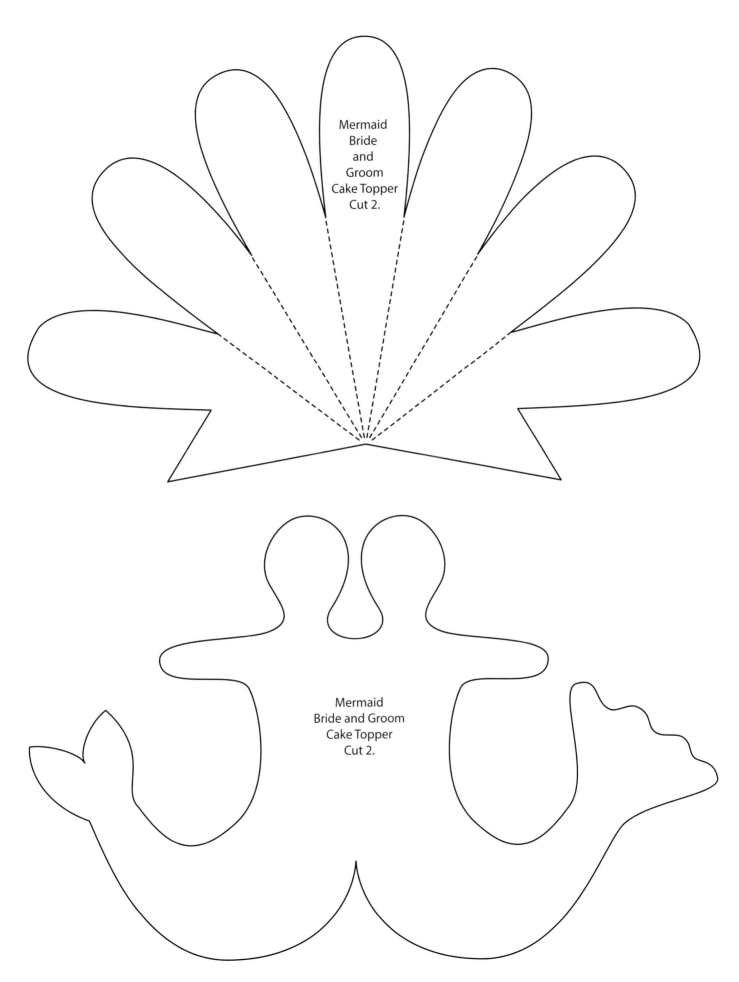

Mermaid
Bride
and
Groom
Cake Topper
Cut 2.

Mermaid
Bride and Groom
Cake Topper
Cut 2.

Angel Tree Topper

Finished size: approximately 5½″ × 5½″ × 11″ ✤ *Refer to Getting Started (pages 7–11).*

What You Need

✤ Basic Supplies, page 11.

✤ 2 pieces 15″ × 18″ (38.1 × 45.7cm) medium-weight fast2fuse (C&T Publishing)

✤ 1 piece 8″ × 18″ (20.3 × 45.7cm) fabric for skirt

✤ 1 piece 8″ × 18″ (20.3 × 45.7cm) fabric for skirt backing

✤ 1 piece 9″ × 14″ (22.9 × 35.6cm) flesh-colored fabric

✤ 2 pieces 11″ × 18″ (27.9 × 45.7cm) fabric for skirt structure

✤ Polyester fiberfill (I use Poly-Fil.)

✤ Embellishments and trim

✤ Fabric or acrylic paints

✤ Fabric markers

Instructions

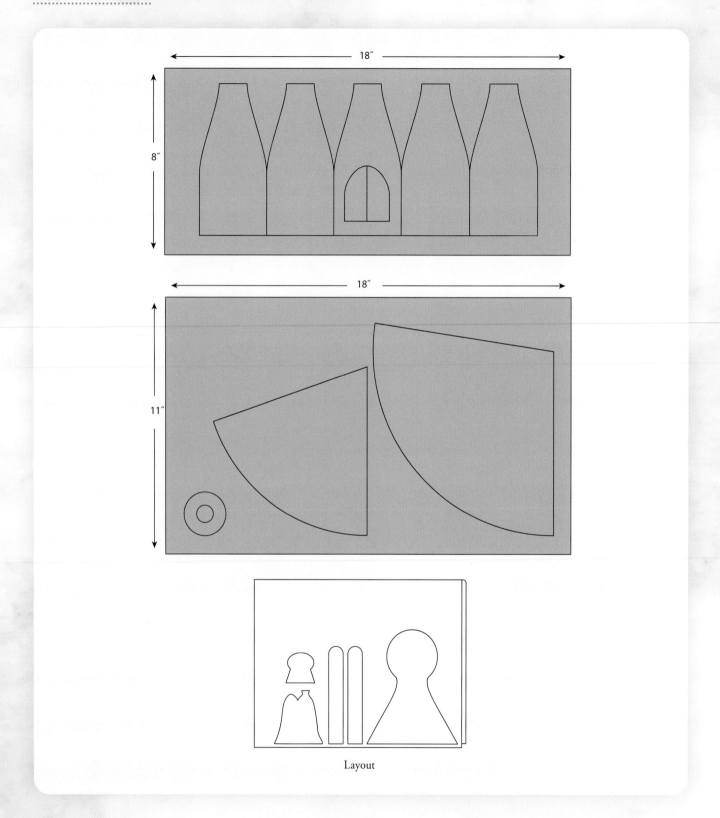

18″

8″

18″

11″

Layout

The Skirt

1. Cut 1 piece of fast2fuse 8″ × 18″ (20.3 × 45.7cm). Using the skirt and skirt backing fabrics, make a fabric sandwich (see Making a Fabric Sandwich, page 9).

2. Trace the skirt pattern piece (page 80) onto the fabric sandwich and cut it out. Mark the lines for the door pieces.

3. Cut out the door and zigzag around the door opening and the 2 door pieces. Paint the backs of the doors, let them dry and reattach them at the sides, so they can swing open.

4. Sew the skirt sections together, one section at a time. I sew them side by side pressing the pieces together at the curves. Join the pieces by sewing the final seam with right sides together. You can also sew all of the pieces right sides together, if that's easier. *figs A–B*

5. Turn the skirt piece right side out by pushing the top through the bottom opening. You have to show it who's boss. It may resist, but in the end, you will win! *fig C*

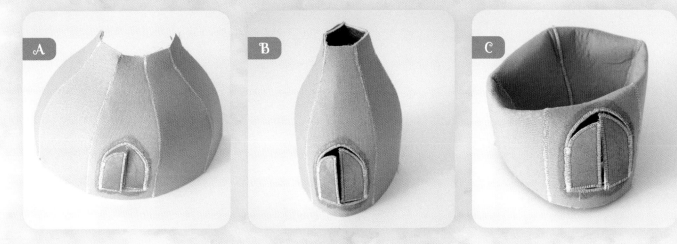

6. Zigzag around the bottom edge of the skirt. This makes the skirt firmer and rounder at the bottom edge. *fig D*

7. Cut a piece of fast2fuse 11″ × 18″ (27.9 × 45.7cm). Make a second fabric sandwich using the skirt structure fabric.

8. Trace the skirt structure and stabilizing circle pattern pieces (page 81) onto the fabric sandwich and cut them out.

9. Sew each skirt structure at the sides to make 2 cone shapes.

10. Paint the larger cone piece since this will be the background for the nativity figures. *fig E*

11. Glue the tip of the small cone inside the larger cone using a glue gun. Place the stabilizing circle onto the tip of the large cone and put the cone inside the skirt to make sure things are fitting together well. The circle will keep the cone in place and needs to fit tightly into the skirt near the top. *figs F–G*

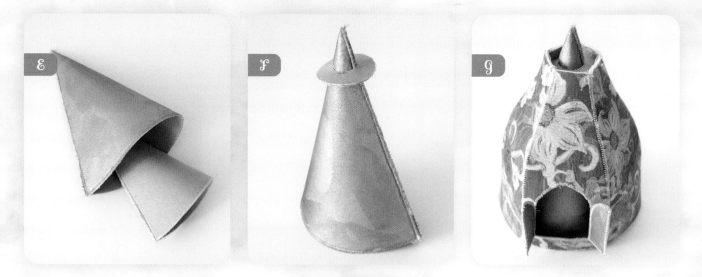

12. Once you are satisfied with the fit, and with the cone still inside the skirt, glue the inner edge of the circle to the cone with the glue gun. Glue the outer edge of the circle to the skirt. This doesn't have to be super neat since it will not show.

The Angel and Nativity Pieces

1. Fold the piece of flesh-colored fabric in half with right sides together. Trace the angel body, arms, and the nativity figures pattern pieces (page 81) onto the fabric but *don't* cut them out yet.

2. Sew just the arms and nativity pieces on the line using a small straight stitch. Trim about ⅛″ (3mm) from the stitched line.

3. Turn the arms right side out. To turn the nativity figures pieces right side out, cut a small slit in one layer of fabric on the back. *figs A–B*

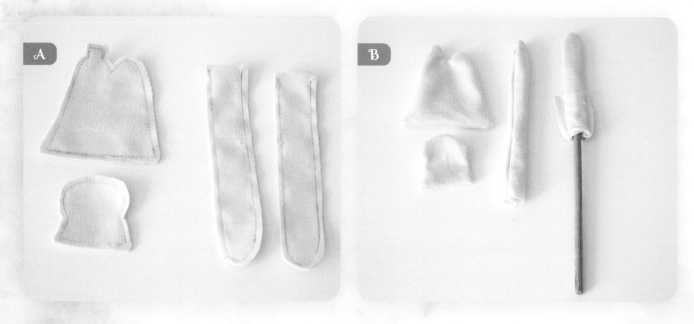

4. Stuff the nativity pieces and hand sew the opening closed. *fig C*

5. Put a little stuffing into the tips of the arms and pin the arms between the layers of the traced body piece. *fig D*

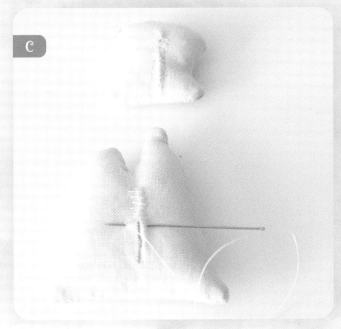

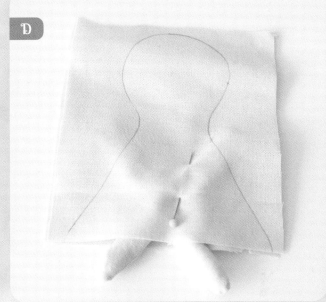

6. Sew the body on the traced line using a small straight stitch, being careful not to move the arms out of place. Turn the body right side out and stuff.

7. Paint the nativity figures pieces. Paint the face and body of the angel.

8. Sew detailing on the nativity pieces to give more definition to the shapes (optional). Decorate the body of the angel. *figs E–F*

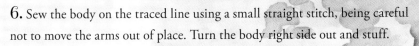

Finishing

1. Position the angel over the skirt, so the edge of the body fabric overlaps the skirt and the center of the face lines up with the center of the door. Using a glue gun, put glue on the top edge of the skirt, under the edge of the angel fabric, and press firmly in place. Glue the back of the body to the skirt in the same manner. *fig A*

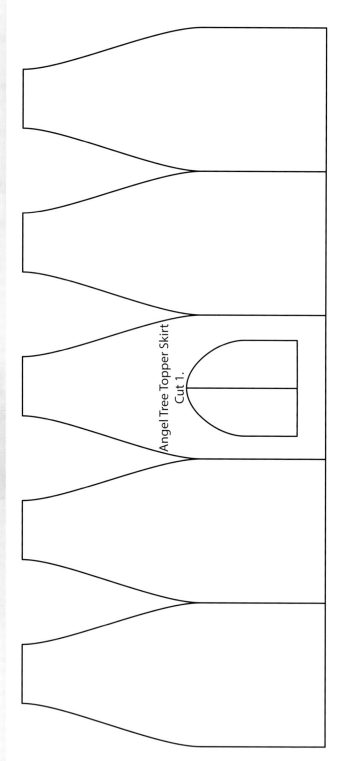

Enlarge skirt pattern 200%.

3. Glue the nativity figures to the cone, inside the door opening, making sure the bottom lines up with the bottom of the door, and that the figures are centered in the opening.

4. Cover the bottom edge of the body with trim to hide the unfinished edge. Glue on the necklace, the hair, the wings, and any other embellishments that are suitable or that you want to add.

5. Glue the hands together in the praying position, making sure no glue is showing on the front, then glue the hands in place.

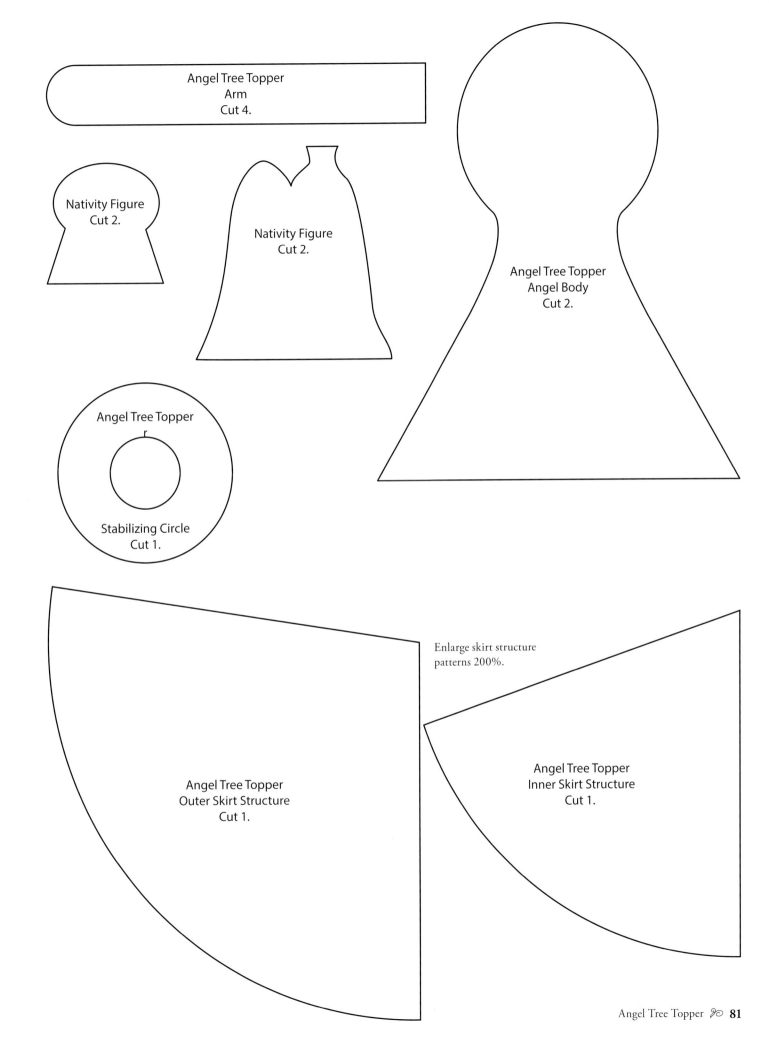

Angel Tree Topper
Arm
Cut 4.

Nativity Figure
Cut 2.

Nativity Figure
Cut 2.

Angel Tree Topper
Angel Body
Cut 2.

Angel Tree Topper
r

Stabilizing Circle
Cut 1.

Angel Tree Topper
Outer Skirt Structure
Cut 1.

Enlarge skirt structure
patterns 200%.

Angel Tree Topper
Inner Skirt Structure
Cut 1.

Nativity Ornament

Finished size: approximately ¾″ × 2¾″ × 4¼″ ✤ *Refer to Getting Started (pages 7–11).*

What You Need

✤ Basic Supplies, page 11.

✤ 1 piece 8″ × 7″ (20.3 × 17.8cm) medium-weight fast2fuse (C&T Publishing)

✤ 1 piece 8″ × 7″ (20.3 × 17.8cm) solid-colored fabric for nativity box interior

✤ 1 piece 8″ × 7″ (20.3 × 17.8cm) print or solid-colored fabric for nativity box exterior

✤ 1 piece 4″ × 10″ (10.2 × 25.4cm) fabric for nativity figures

✤ Polyester fiberfill (I use Poly-Fil.)

✤ Fabric or acrylic paints

✤ Fabric markers

✤ Tiny glass star bead

✤ String for hanging (optional)

Instructions

Nativity Box

1. Make a fabric sandwich using the fast2fuse and the nativity box fabrics (see Making a Fabric Sandwich, page 9).

2. Trace the nativity pattern piece (page 85) onto the fabric sandwich. Mark the cutting lines separating the sections and door.

3. Cut out the shape. Cut out the door and separate the side sections.

4. Zigzag around the door opening and the doors.

5. Reattach the doors at the sides, so they can swing open. Reattach the side sections. *fig A*

6. Sew the corners of the box together, folding and crushing the box down so you can line up the edges. *fig B*

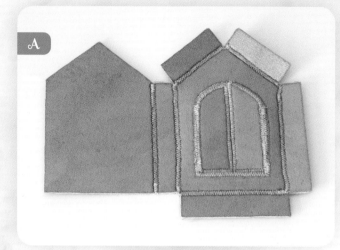

7. Hand sew or glue the back piece.

8. Sew a tiny glass star bead onto the top front of the box. *fig C*

Nativity Figures

1. Fold the nativity fabric in half with right sides together and trace the figure (page 81) onto the fabric. Sew on the line using a small straight stitch. Trim about ⅛″ (3mm) from the stitched line.

2. Cut a small slit through one layer of fabric in the back of the figures and turn them inside out.

3. Stuff the figures and hand sew the opening closed.

4. Decorate the front of the figures. Sew a seam down the middle with a small straight stitch to separate the figures. *fig D*

5. Glue the figures inside the box (this is so cute!).

Note ◡
If you want to use this as an ornament, attach a string to the back at the top of the box.

Nativity Ornament
Cut 1.

Happy Birthday Cake

Finished size: approximately 5″ × 5″ × 5½″   ✤   *Refer to Getting Started (pages 7–11).*

What You Need (make one slice)

✤ Basic Supplies, page 11.

✤ 1 piece 15″ × 18″ (38.1 × 45.7cm) medium-weight fast2fuse (C&T Publishing)

✤ 8″ × 11″ (20.3 × 27.9cm) fabric for cake slice sides (brown)

✤ 8″ × 11″ (20.3 × 27.9cm) fabric for cake slice sides backing

✤ 8″ × 10″ (20.3 × 25.4cm) fabric for cake slice top/bottom and filling (purple)

✤ 6″ × 10″ (15.2 × 25.4cm) fabric for cake slice top/bottom backing

✤ 7″ × 8″ (17.8 × 20.3cm) fabric for cake side (berry)

✤ 7″ × 8″ (17.8 × 20.3cm) fabric for cake side backing

✤ Tiny safety pin

✤ Ruler

✤ Base for candle (I use a carton from eggs) (optional)

✤ 8″ (20.3cm) LuxuryLite LED taper candle and remote control (optional)

✤ Embellishments

Instructions

1. Cut 1 strip 2″ × 10″ (5.1 × 25.4cm) of the purple cake slice top fabric and set it aside. Use the remaining 6″ × 10″ (15.2 × 25.4cm) for the fabric sandwich.

2. Cut the fast2fuse into 3 sizes: 8″ × 11″ (20.3 × 27.9cm) for the cake slice sides, 6″ × 10″ (15.2 × 25.4cm) for the cake slice top/bottom, and 7″ × 8″ (17.8 × 20.3cm) for the cake side. Using the corresponding fabrics to make 3 fabric sandwiches (see Making a Fabric Sandwich, page 9).

3. Trace the pattern pieces for the cake slice side, cake slice top/bottom, and cake side (page 90) and cut them out. Mark the lines on the slice side piece.

4. Cut the strip from Step 1 in half lengthwise to make 2 strips 1″ × 10″ (2.5 × 25.4cm). Fold the strips in half lengthwise with right sides together and sew about ⅛″ (3mm) from the raw edges using a medium straight stitch.

5. Turn the strips right side out by attaching a tiny safety pin to one end of the strip going through only one thickness of the fabric. Gently push the safety pin through the fabric tube until it comes out the other end. Press the strips, so they are flat, keeping the seam in the middle of the strip. *fig A*

6. Place the purple strips on the marked lines on the brown slice side pieces. Topstitch on each side of the strip close to the fold.

7. Cut on the lines to separate the brown tab sections. Cut the shape down the middle to make the point of the slice. *fig B*

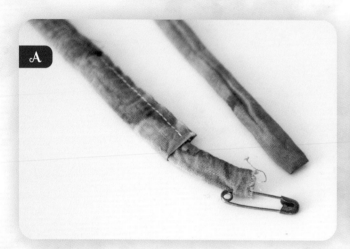

8. Reattach the tabs using a zigzag stitch. Sew the slice side pieces to the berry cake side piece. *fig C*

9. If you plan to use the candle, cut a round opening in one of the cake slice triangles, and mark the circle on the inside of the other triangle, so you know where to glue the base for the candle. *Make sure that the candle fits easily inside the opening in the top piece before going to the next step.* Zigzag around the opening as well as the edges. *fig D*

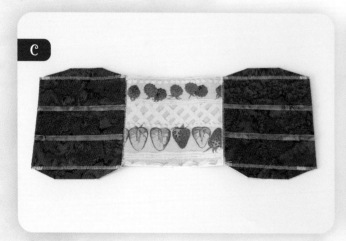

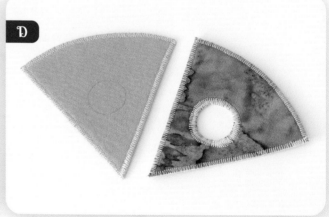

10. Sew the curved edge of the purple cake slice triangle piece to the cake side piece. Since one shape is curved and the other one is straight, you will have to gently press the edges together as you sew them side by side.

Tip

I pick the pieces up at the sides and hold them together as I sew. You'll find that they easily glide through the presser foot. The sides of the 2 pieces that are getting sewn together will lift off the sewing surface to accommodate the curve. Just let them do that and it flows perfectly together.

11. Sew the bottom cake slice triangle the same way. If using the candle, glue the candle base onto the marked circle with the glue gun. This is the best time to sew any beads onto the side piece since it's harder to do after the pieces are joined. *fig E*

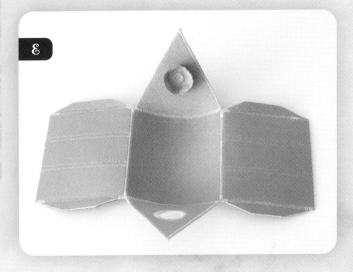

12. With the wrong sides together, zigzag the slice side pieces together on the edge, making sure that the needle lands just off the fabrics on the outer edge and through both thicknesses on the inner edge.

13. Using your hands, reshape the cake slice by opening up the seam at the point, so the cake sides are nice and straight. *fig F*

14. Fold the tabs inside the cake slice and carefully glue or hand sew the bottom triangle to the tabs, making sure that the tabs don't show. Decorate the top of the cake with the embellishments and glue or hand sew the top cake slice triangle in place. *fig G*

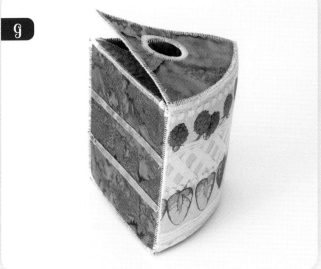

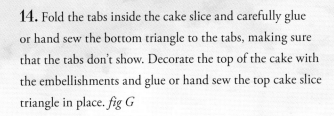

Happy Birthday Cake
Cake Slice Top/Bottom
Cut 2.

Happy Birthday Cake
Cake Side
Cut 1.

Enlarge cake patterns 200%

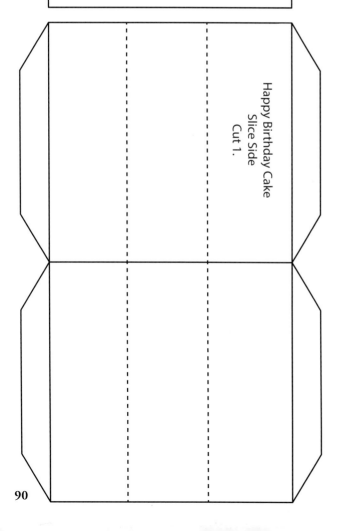

Happy Birthday Cake
Slice Side
Cut 1.

15. Make a total of 6 cake slices to complete your cake.

If you are using the candle, it will fit right into the hole and sit nicely on the base inside the cake. *fig H*

H

Gallery

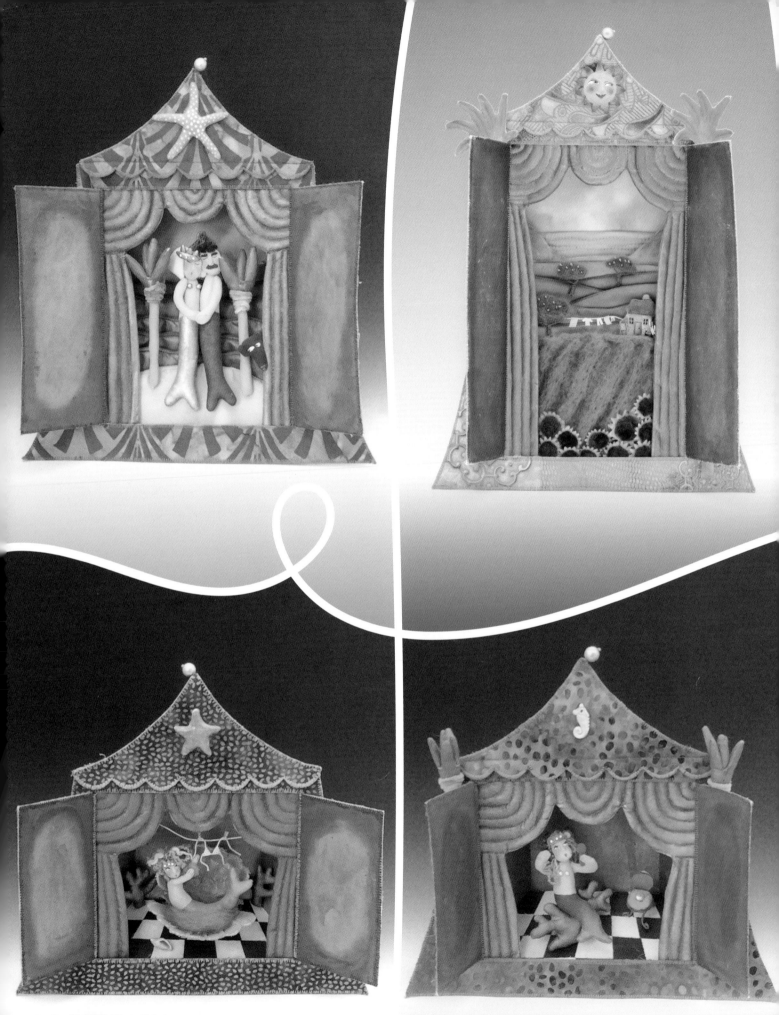